Custer's Chief of Scouts

CADET CHARLES VARNUM
West Point, Class of 1872
Courtesy, U.S. Military Academy
Archives

LT. COL. CHARLES VARNUM
A photograph from c. 1905
Courtesy U.S. Military Academy
Archives

Custer's Chief of Scouts

The Reminiscences of Charles A. Varnum

Including his testimony at the
Reno Court of Inquiry

Edited by
John M. Carroll

Introduction and
Biographical Chronology by
Charles K. Mills

University of Nebraska Press
Lincoln and London

First Bison Book printing: 1987
Most recent printing indicated by the first digit below:
1   2   3   4   5   6   7   8   9   10

Library of Congress Cataloging-in-Publication Data
Varnum, Charles Albert, 1849–1936.
    Custer's chief of scouts.

    Previously published as: I, Varnum. Glendale, Calif.:
A. H. Clark, 1982. (Hidden springs of Custeriana; 7).
    Includes index.
    1. Varnum, Charles Albert, 1849–1936. 2. Soldiers—
United States—Biography. 3. United States. Army.
Cavalry, 7th—Biography. 4. Indians of North America—
Wars—1866–1895—Personal narratives. 5. Little Big
Horn, Battle of the, 1876—Personal narratives.
6. Reno, Marcus A. (Marcus Albert), 1835–1889.
I. Carroll, John M. (John Melvin), 1928–   .
II. Title.
E83.866.V274 1987   357'.1'0924 [B]   87-6054
ISBN 0-8032-1441-3
ISBN 0-8032-6328-7 (pbk.)

Reprinted by arrangement with John M. Carroll

In Memory of Mike's Maggie

Contents

Illustrations

Acknowledgements

I wish to thank Joseph Rubinfine for allowing this manuscript to be published. Charles K. Mills must be complimented on his fine Introduction and the chronological documentation on the life of Varnum. Without the aid of the National Archives, especially Dr. Elaine Everly, nothing can be truly accomplished in the field of frontier military history. And finally, West Point, Robert Utley, the Custer Battlefield, and especially Dr. Lawrence Frost must be recognized for their generosity in making photographs of Varnum available for this publication.

Introduction

Charles Albert Varnum wore his country's uniform for over fifty years: first the cadet gray of West Point, then the familiar blue of a 7th Cavalry officer, and finally the khaki-brown of the twentieth century Army. Varnum was just a few months past his nineteenth birthday when he first swore an oath to defend the country of his birth, and was just weeks shy of his seventieth year when he was relieved of that responsibility. He lived well over halfway through his eighty-seventh year and could look back on a life that was not only unusually long, but one that was filled with events that rarely are experienced by a single individual except in fictional epics. When Varnum was born, Zachary Taylor, the hero of the Mexican War, was president and horses were the primary means of transportation. When he died, Franklin D. Roosevelt was gearing up to run for a second term and all-metal airplanes zoomed across the skies.

Born on the 21st of June 1849 in Troy, New York, Charles was the son of John Varnum – one of an unusually large clan of Varnums who resided in or near Dracut, Massachusetts. The first Varnum to come to this country – George Varnum – came to what is now Ipswich, Massachusetts with his wife and two children in 1635. Originally, the Varnums were Welsh, but by the mid-nineteenth century when Charles Albert was born, they were almost entirely of English stock. Varnum's mother was named Nancy E. Green. There were five children in his family: two sisters, and three brothers. And, while a five-child household was not unusual for mid-nineteenth century America, the Varnums were part of a family where large numbers of children were the rule rather than the exception. On the subject of ancestry, two generals during the Revolutionary War were named Varnum and, apparently, they were uncles of Charles A. Varnum's great-grandfather, Prescot Varnum.

As related in the autobiography, Charles Varnum moved to his ancestral home – Dracut, Massachusetts – when he was two-years-old and grew up there. His father, a Union Army officer, ended the war in Florida and the family joined him in Pensacola in 1866. For this reason, Varnum, a seventh generation Massachusetts man, was appointed to West Point from Florida in 1868.

He did well at the Academy. Aside from a court-martial in 1871 for the seemingly trivial offense of "deserting his post" as a cadet sentry, he did quite well. He graduated seventeenth in a class of fifty-seven in June 1872. His room-mate and best friend, George D. "Nick" Wallace of South Carolina, did even better and may have provided some help, if it were needed. Varnum did well enough, smart room-mate or none. He was appointed as a Second Lieutenant to the 7th Cavalry, then scattered throughout the South on mounted police duty.

In July 1872, before he had used up his graduation leave in Florida, he was assigned to Company A, commanded by Captain Myles Moylan and stationed – with the regimental headquarters – at Elizabethtown, Kentucky. Varnum's slot had recently been vacated by the promotion of Francis M. Gibson to the first lieutenancy of H Company.

His autobiography details his service in the South and the subsequent move to the Dakotas in 1873. Furthermore, the Stanley Yellowstone Expedition, the Black Hills Expedition of 1874, the brief re-deployment of a portion of the regiment to the South, and the Little Big Horn campaign of 1876 are also well-described. Varnum added very little in the way of his own opinions about his fellow officers – with one exception, and a rather indirect one at that. The precise reason for his extreme dislike of Marcus A. Reno is not given, but the conventional wisdom is that Reno's poor showing on 25 June 1876 was exacerbated by the outstanding performances of some of the junior officers such as Varnum, Wallace, and Hare. Captain Frederick W. Benteen, a man not noted for his charitable assessments of his fellow officers, told a corresondent years later that "had I anything to say in the matter, I should have recommended for brevets, first Hare, then Varnum, and lastly, Godfrey, yes Wallace, too, before Hare, then I think I should have stopped." (Benteen-Goldin, 19 October 1894)

But, Varnum was *not* breveted for the Little Big Horn and the student of the battle must wonder why. Varnum tells why in relating his conversation with Reno on the night of the 25th. He had approached the Major, suggested that he and Sergeant Culbertson be permitted to ride for help, and argued when Reno refused permission. When Varnum persisted, Reno fixed him with a baleful stare and said: "Varnum, you are a very uncomfortable companion." That single statement – with all that it implied and suggests even now –

is the most important clue to Varnum's character revealed in the writing. Stalwartness, valor, devotion to duty in the face of overwhelming odds, pluck, courage, and so forth all have ways of making lesser mortals feel "uncomfortable" in the company of men – like Varnum – who possess these traits.

As Varnum relates, he was given command of the provisional troop that was formed from the survivors, stretching the seven companies to eight for the balance of the campaign. Upon his return to Fort Lincoln, he assumed command of Comany C, formerly commanded by Captain Tom Custer. The night the 7th arrived at Lincoln, there was a "blow-out" at the Officer's Club and Varnum felt constrained to intervene in a fist fight between a drunken Reno and an infantry lieutenant named Manly. Reno threatened to kill Varnum and summoned up the worst insult he could possibly direct at a young officer anxious to establish a military reputation.

Not surprisingly, Varnum had very little use for Major Reno, for these and other reasons, long after the latter was dead and gone. Yet, out of a sense of loyalty to the regiment, he refrained from publicly attacking Reno and, when given the opportunity to testify at the Reno Court of Inquiry in 1879, avoided giving damaging testimony. It is interesting to speculate about just how "comfortable" Reno might have felt when Varnum was in the witness's chair.

The remainder of his career to 1890 reads like a potted biography of a fictional hero in a second-rate Western. The only difference, of course, is that in Varnum's case it was anything but bad fiction. He was asked to remain with C Company long after Captain Henry

Jackson assumed command to "help" whip the company into shape. He was detailed to do the same for I Company temporarily. He was asked to assume the duties of regimental quartermaster when another officer refused to work for the new colonel. He was active in recruiting and training Indian scouts (a legitimate function of a quartermaster in the frontier Army) and he seemed to excel in this duty. He was sent to H Company in the spring of 1880 to allow its company commanders to take some time off for detached service and he commanded the famous H Company (H Troop after 1883) off and on for the next ten years.

In the summer of 1890, Tom McDougall finally retired and Varnum was promoted to Captain and given command of Mac's B Troop. It was in this capacity that he went to Wounded Knee. He and his friend Nick Wallace were the officers detailed to search the Miniconjou lodges and Varnum was standing beside Major Whitside when the guns went off. The next day, at White Clay Creek, he ignored an ill-advised order to abandon his position and, at great personal risk, led a charge that recaptured higher ground and allowed the other troops present to extricate themselves without further loss. Seven years later, he was awarded the nation's highest award for valor, the Medal of Honor, for this deed.

He continued to command B Troop for ten years, leading them to Ft. Sheridan (near Chicago) to act as railroad police during the labor troubles of the '90s. He spent three years as professor of military science at the University of Wyoming, rejoining his B Troop just as they were embarking for Cuba during the Spanish-American War. He lasted less than six months in the malarial tropics of Cuba before being sent home for a prolonged medical treatment and leave of absence. He was sent on detached service to Denver as much for his health as anything else while his B Troop remained in Cuba. It was in Denver, in 1901, that the fifty-one-year-old Captain Varnum was given a long overdue promotion to Major. Two years later, he rejoined the 7th in Georgia. After a year and a half as the senior major of the 7th Cavalry in Georgia, he was transferred to the Negro 9th Cavalry, commanded by his old comrade Edward S. Godfrey. After just six months with the 9th, Varnum was promoted to Lieutenant Colonel and transferred to the 4th Cavalry, stationed on the West Coast. He went to the Philippines with his new regiment, commanding the base at Malabang for a year and a half before being ordered home for retirement.

On 31 October 1907, Varnum was retired from the Regular Army for disability incurred in the line of duty. But, even after thirty-five years as a Regular Army officer, at the age of 58, he wasn't ready to hang up his uniform. He remained on active duty, first as an advisor to the Idaho Militia, then as a professor of military science at the University of Maine, and finally as a recruiting officer. In July 1918, at the height of American mobilization for the First World War, he was promoted to Colonel and made disbursing officer at Fort Mason in San Francisco.

And there he remained until his release from active duty on 8 April 1919.

He outlived all the 1876 7th Cavalry officers and all but a handful of the enlisted men. He even outlived Libbie Custer, who lived into her nineties. On 26 February 1936, Charles Albert Varnum died in a hospital in the Presidio. He was survived by his wife, Mary Alice, and by his daughter, Georgie. On the day he died, just four months shy of his eighty-seventh birthday, the newspaper headlines blared that the Japanese Army had staged a *coup* in Tokyo, a foreshadowing of the inevitable World War II.

Unfortunately, Varnum's autobiography is far from complete, but it does provide an interesting insight into the experiences of a man whose name became almost synonymous with valor, a man who served in the 7th Cavalry for thirty-two years, a man who – unlike most others – emerged from the Little Big Horn debacle untainted by controversy.

CHARLES K. MILLS
Tucson, Arizona

Foreword

I had always considered the two most closed-mouthed officers of the 7th U. S. Cavalry to be Charles Varnum and Luther Hare. Both seemed reluctant to talk about themselves, Custer or the Battle of the Little Big Horn. They avoided print and in general just ignored or forgot the historic events on the frontier. Both testified at the Reno Court of Inquiry, and but for an occasional comment or two to the press, that was that.

Today, however, only Luther Hare can claim that distinction. To my knowledge, no narrative of any consequence authored by Luther Hare has ever surfaced, but within the past few months, not one, but two narratives by Varnum have. The first was a short account authored by retired Colonel T. M. Coughlan which had been based upon a series of interviews with the eighty-six-year old Varnum. On this it can be assumed the interviews transpired during the 1930s, but never found publication – that despite its apparent value as a truly human document. When I discovered the manuscript, a concluding page was missing, perhaps more, for there was no way of ascertaining the extent of the narrative; both parties were deceased. I printed what was there in 1980, along with some short additional material, in a pamphlet in an edition of only fifty copies. It was entitled simply *Varnum*.

Then some few months later another manuscript surfaced, and this unfinished manuscript, like the other with pages missing, was clearly the beginning of an

I, Varnum

autobiography, short though it was. However this time I knew where it ended, for the missing pages were toward the end of the manuscript, but not at the conclusion. In my transcription I made the statement it was never finished, suggesting without foundation, that more had been anticipated, but Varnum died before its completion. More's the pity! for Varnum seemed to speak (write) straight from the shoulder, a rare commodity in most autobiographies.

It is a pity the two manuscripts were not discovered at the same time and somehow combined, for there are many interesting facts in the published manuscript which were not included in this one.

For instance, Varnum relates a few first-hand incidents of the Nez Perce Campaign. One such incident comes to mind: General Sturgis was ordered to intercept the Nez Perce Indians as they issued from the Yellowstone Park area. Chief Joseph eluded his and General Howard's forces as they fled down Clark's Fork of the Yellowstone, and northward to Canada. The troops were then faced with the unmistakable and ever present danger of being without food, especially as they were to pursue the Indians as directed. Varnum describes the situation thusly:

> Beset with marauding bands of savages, over rugged trails in uncharted mountain wilds; in the stifling heat of the Montana sun on the limb-blasting cold of snow-laden winter, these indomitable groups of men and horses plodded on and on to the call of duty. Adding to these hardships was the uncertainty of the fighting columns. Plans for rendezvous would be made only to be broken; orders countermanded and contact between the troops and the trains entirely dependent upon the hazard of messenger service. One night during the combat near Clark's Fork, an Indian courier slipped into my camp with a letter from Colo-

nel Sturgis to General Howard. Recognizing the hand writing,
I opened it and learned that Sturgis' command was living on
mule meat.

His narrative continued, relating how he had Sturgis'
wounded in his camp and how he loaded them up and
started for the Yellowstone. It was there he found a
boat loaded with potatoes and onions, purchased the
cargo and chartered the vessel.

It was here Varnum ran into Calamity Jane who had
started on her way to the Montana settlements near Fort
Shaw by stage, as "Captain Grant Marsh wouldn't let
her ride on his steamer." The Nez Perces had caused
her to take to the brush, and she was practically naked
when Varnum's men rescued and cared for her. Varnum relates how he "saw her wearing soldier clothes."
Varnum put his wounded on the *Far West,* and arranged with Captain Marsh to allow Calamity Jane
to ride on his steamer as a nurse to Fort Yates. "Then
and for many years after the soldiers expressed their
enthusiasm of her nursing in the highest of terms."

Once the wounded were taken care of, Varnum
loaded wagons with the food and hurried to the relief
of Sturgis and his command. After that, and after the
surrender of Chief Joseph, Varnum led his wagon train
to his post at Fort Abraham Lincoln.

In Sturgis' official report of the 1877 Campaign, he
cited Varnum as follows: "The skill and zeal with
which our supply train was managed by my Regimental Quartermaster, throughout the whole campaign,
entitles that faithful officer to special commendation."

Varnum also related in the previously published
manuscript his participation in the Wounded Knee
affair in December 1890:

I, Varnum

Early in December word was received that Big Foot, noted Indian Chief, having surrendered to General Sumner, had escaped with his band of Ogallala Sioux and was moving south through the Bad Lands. Major Whitside, sent with four troops to head them off, camped December 27th near the mouth of Wounded Knee Creek, emptying into the White River. Next morning the Indians were seen lined up on a ridge. A parley ensued. My Troop B and K Troop were dismounted in line with the other two troops, mounted, behind them. As the Indians came in their impudent and truculent attitude warned me to have my men load their rifles. This temporarily checked the impending clash as the soldiers forcibly prevented them from kicking over a small howitzer. They agreed to go into camp. Here I learned that Big Foot was suffering from pneumonia, and I placed him and his squaw in a tent near the scout's lines. The Indian ponies were turned out to graze. On his arrival in camp, Whitside had sent to Pine Ridge agency for reinforcements and that night, Colonel Forsyth arrived with four more troops of the regiment. The following morning a council was called and it was decided to secure the arms. A search of the camp by myself and Wallace disclosed but one rifle.

Varnum advised Whitside that he believed the Indians had their guns under their blankets. Whitside then told the men to go ahead with the search. The rest is history. Varnum:

In order to picture the dramatic action that followed, a word of explanation is necessary. Drawn up on the banks of a dry branch was the long Indian line formed in a flat arc, facing the line of the two dismounted troops about fifteen yards away. The squaws and children in the far rear. It was bitterly cold. The warriors' blankets covered them completely, exposing only their eyes. My first sergeant and I, with a few men, started the search of the left of the line. The first Indian stood up, threw open his blanket showing a belt full of cartridges, but no gun. As I was turning to secure a receptacle for the cartridges, the entire hostile line rose to their feet as one man, turned their backs, shook off their blankets and turning again with the hidden rifles in their hands fired a volley point blank at the troops. The latter was ready, for there was but one deafening crash as Indians and soldiers fired together. The surrounding troops joined the melee as soon as it began. The hostile line wilted and the few survivors disappeared over the bank into the ravine. Unwittingly that one volley of the troops swept through the village and doubtless killed many women and children. Big Foot fell in the cross-fire and I lost my lifelong chum, Captain Wallace, who met his death in the brush where he had gone searching for arms. The toll was heavy on both sides. My troop alone sustained a loss of four killed and seven wounded.

As in almost all episodes of combat there is something, afterwards, one can look upon and laugh, or at least smile. Wounded Knee was no exception. Throughout the fight, Varnum steadfastly clutched the stem of his old pipe between his teeth. The bowl was gone, neatly shot from his mouth, and not noticed until after the fight. For his action in this engagement, Varnum was awarded the Medal of Honor:

. . . While executing an order to withdraw, seeing that a continuance of movement would expose another troop of his regiment to being cut off and surrounded, he disregarded orders to retire, placed himself in front of his men, led a charge upon the advancing Indians, regained a commanding position that had just been vacated and then insured a safe withdrawal of both detachments without further loss.

In a short interview Varnum had granted Charles Bates, the following statements by Varnum were made concerning the Little Big Horn campaign:

There has been much speculation about what I feel sure was a bit of pleasantry on the part of General Gibbon. As the entire Seventh Cavalry passed General Terry in review on the 22nd . . . General Gibbon said to General Custer as he bade him goodbye, "Don't be greedy Custer, leave some for us," or words to that effect. Many years afterwards this was brought up as an additional evidence that Custer was disposed to upset the carefully laid plans. An officer asked Gibbon one day what he meant by this "greedy" remark. Gibbon replied, "I meant nothing in that except that I wanted Custer to know that I knew he was always ready to fight and that I wanted him to know that if there was anything I could do, I was ready and willing to do it. . . ."

I am satisfied that the whole plan was a pursuit plan which is the keynote of General Terry's letter of instructions dated June 22nd. It might be described as a cowboy round-up of Indians.

I have seen a photostat copy of a letter dated June 21 written in pencil by Captain George Yates who was killed . . . In this letter Captain Yates states what he thinks the plan will be . . . [It] was almost the same in general effect as the longer and more formal letter of instructions . . . of General Terry. It seemed to me a carte blanche letter of instructions to act on his own initiative and at his own discretion.

It is interesting – to me at least – the repeated reference to Terry's "letter of instructions." I have never viewed his letter as an order, but instructions only, and upon this definition much has been written and argued. Hopefully the use of the word "instructions" by an officer *who was there* will help dispel the question once and for all.

I think the rate of march from the Rosebud at its junction with the Yellowstone was a very moderate march, and I think Lt. Wallace's statement of the length of the marches up to sundown or retreat on the afternoon of the 24th, was accurate. In that period there was no march of 45 miles or anything like it.

I must have been on fairly intimate terms with General Custer for he was the kind of man who kept officers at a distance as a rule. He looked the part of an officer always, but I suppose that I had been in two pretty sharp Indian fights in 1873 under him, and that therefore I had gotten into a relationship that made him lenient with what he would have regarded as impudence on

SEVENTH CAVALRY OFFICERS AND WIVES, 1873

Posed in front of Custer's Quarters at Fort Lincoln, Varnum is indicated by the arrow.

Courtesy, Custer Battlefield National Monument

SEVENTH CAVALRY OFFICERS AFTER WOUNDED KNEE BATTLE. PHOTO TAKEN JANUARY 1891 AT PINE RIDGE. Standing, left to right: Capt. John van R. Hoff, 1st Lt. Loyd S. McCormick, 2d Lt. Sedgwick Rice, 1st Lt. William J. Nicholson, 2d Lt. Selah R. H. Tompkins, 1st. Lt. Horation G. Sickel, Jr., 2d Lt. Joseph E. Maxfield, 2d Lt. James Franklin Bell, Dr. Daniel LeMay, 1st Lt. Edwin P. Brewer, 1st Lt. Jerbert G. Squiers, 1st Lt. Ezra B. Fuller, 1st Lt. John C. Gresham, 1st Lt. William W. Robinson, Jr. Seated on stools, left to right: Capt. Winfield S. Edgerly, Capt. Charles S. Ilsley, Capt. Henry Jackson, Major Samuel M. Whitside, Col. James W. Forsyth, Capt. Myles Moylan, Capt. Henry J. Nowlan, Capt. Edward S. Godfrey. Seated on ground, left to right: Capt. Charles A. Varnum, 2d Lt. Thomas Q. Donaldson, 2d Lt. John C. Waterman.

Courtesy, Col. William M. Pond Collection

CHARLES A. VARNUM
After several years in the
7th Cavalry, a mature officer
Courtesy, George Nas

(left to right)
CHARLES A. VARNUM
NELSON BRONSON
FREDERICK W. BENTEEN
BENJAMIN HODGSON
Courtesy, Custer Battlefield
National Monument

PINE RIDGE, 1891, SHORTLY AFTER WOUNDED KNEE
Seated, left to right: Capt. W.S. Edgerly, Capt. Henry J. Nowlan, Capt. Charles S. Ilsley, Capt. Charles A. Varnum Col. James W. Forsyth, Maj. Samuel W. Whiteside, Capt. Myles Moylan, Capt. Edward S. Godfrey, unidentified.
Courtesy, Graybill Collection, Library of Congress

the part of some officers who did not know him so well. I mention this because it shows that Custer's spirits were far from being depressed on the eve of the big disaster.

(This in reference to Varnum chiding Wallace to go with him and not stay with the coffee coolers.)

These gratuitous remarks and observations are inserted only because they are of and from one who knew Custer, who fought with Custer, and they brush upon subjects that have often been debated, privately and in the press.

The balance of Varnum's public and personal life are outlined by Charles Mills in both his Introduction and the Chronological Outline of Varnum's life. They are invaluable as guides to the researcher who may be interested in one man who served his country on many hostile frontiers.

JOHN M. CARROLL
Bryan, Texas

I, Varnum

I was born in Troy, New York, June 21st, 1849. My father moved to Dracut, Mass. when I was two years old, and I was educated there in the public schools – District No. 7 – and private school of Mr. Phillips at the Center's Meeting House vestry.[1]

During the Civil War I had to work to help support myself as my father was absent in the Army & we seldom heard from him. I, with my mother and two sisters and two brothers,[2] went to Florida in January 1866, to join my father, who was Captain 82d U. S. Colored Infantry,[3] and stationed at Fort Pickens,[4] Pensacola Harbor. I went to work for a Mr. Thayer [5] at the Fort tending store in a little sutler store.

---

[1] Mr. Josiah S. Phillips, in 1860, taught a private school for several terms in the vestry of the Old Yellow Meeting House in Dracut. (Silas R. Coburn, *History of Dracut, Massachusetts,* n.p., 1922, p. 232.)

[2] Of these four, only one sister has been identified – Mary E. Varnum, born 22 April 1847. (Letter to the editor from C. K. Mills, 27 Oct. 1981.)

[3] Actually designated as 82nd U. S. Colored Troops, organized on 4 April 1864, from the 10th Corps de Afrique. They were later consolidated with the 80th U. S. Colored Troops, 6 July 1864, to form the 79th U. S. Colored Troops. That same month they were reorganized and consolidated with the 97th and 99th U. S. Colored Troops, and finally mustered out on 10 Sept. 1866. They served in Louisiana, Florida and Alabama. (Frederick H. Dyer, *A Compendium of the Records of the War of the Rebellion,* 1908, p. 1736.)

[4] Fort Pickens was located on the western tip of Santa Rosa Island commanding the eastern entrance of Pensacola Harbor. Construction was begun in 1828, and the post was first garrisoned in Oct. 1834. The post was not regularly garrisoned and the last report of troops at the fort was in 1867. (Francis P. Prucha, *A Guide to the Military Posts of the United States, 1789-1895,* Madison, Wisc., 1964, p. 97.)

[5] No record of the sutler, Mr. Thayer, could be found, though because of the time frame involved, Mr. Thayer could possibly have been involved in the purchase of post traderships, a wide-spread practice of the day.

I, Varnum

In going to Florida we sailed from Boston to New
Orleans, and thence by steamer, *N. P. Banks*,[6] to Barrancas Barracks,[7] Pensacola Harbor, & then by open
boat across the bay to Fort Pickens.

My father's regiment was consolidated at Fort Pickens in June or July before going to New Orleans to
be mustered out of service, but before the consolidation
I saw the store and ran it until the troops left in August,
to a good profit. My family remained at Pickens while
my father was absent at New Orleans, and moved over
to Barrancas when he returned after muster out & where
he was employed for some time in the Quartermaster
Department. During his absence I obtained the appointment of Paymaster Clerk, N. S. Steamer, *Tallapoosa*,[8] U. S. Navy, with Paymaster Frank H. Arms,[9]
appointment date August 18th, 1866.

The Gulf Squadron under Admiral Winslow [10] was

---

[6] The *N. P. Banks* was the *General Nathanial P. Banks,* an army transport.

[7] Barrancas Barracks was a three-story brick building, situated on a sand
plateau overlooking the Bay of Pensacola, Santa Rosa Island, and the Gulf
of Mexico, about 470 yards distant from the garrison of Fort Barrancas.
(Asst. Surg. Gen. John S. Billings, *Report on Hygiene of the United States
Army With Descriptions of Military Posts,* War Dept. Surg. Gen. Office, Circular No. 8, Wash., D.C., 1875, p. 115.) Fort Barrancas was originally built
by the Spanish at the west side of the entrance to Pensacola Harbor, and was
first occupied by U. S. troops on 21 Oct. 1820. The fort was seized by Confederate troops in 1861, but recaptured by U. S. troops in 1862. The fort
was not regularly used after the Civil War, as the troops were garrisoned
at the Barracks.

[8] The *Tallapoosa* was a wooded, sidewheel steamer built during the Civil
War.

[9] The *General Navy Register,* page 27, cites Frank H. Arms as Act. Asst.
Paymaster on 14 April 1864, and by 14 Oct. 1871 was Paymaster.

[10] Rear Adm. John A. Winslow, cited in *General Navy Register,* p. 598.
Although he would not have been a rear admiral on the date Varnum arrived,
this narrative was written in later years, and he respectfully referred to the
gentleman at the highest rank he held, much like the Army used brevet ranks
in reference and respect.

rendevouzed at Pensacola at this time. The *Tallapoosa* was ordered to Galveston, Texas, and from there down on the Mexican coast, then back to Galveston, and we returned from there convoying the *Paul Jones*,[11] and arrived in Pensacola Harbor on January 1867. As the *Tallapoosa* was to go north & out of commission, I took my discharge March 31st, 1867, and went home to Warrington, Florida, just outside the Navy Yard.

Soon after this I was to work for the quartermaster at Barrancas Barracks in connection with the construction of a national cemetery and removal of the remains of fallen soldiers of the Civil War thereto. During the reconstruction period '67-'68, I was Clerk of the Board of Registration of Voters under U. S. Army direction, and afterwards Clerk of Elections at the first election, and in July 1868, I received an appointment at West Point and was ordered to report there August 28th, 1868.

As the railroad had been partly destroyed during the war, I rode 18 miles out of Pensacola by rail, then staged it to Polland, Ala., & then bought tickets from place to place and arrived in Washington via steamboat from Quantico, Va. I went to Lowell, Mass. and stayed about a month studying for my examination, and then to West Point, where I graduated June 14th, 1872, No. 17 in a class of 57 members & was recommended for promotion in Artillery, Cavalry and Infantry.[12]

---

[11] The *Paul Jones* referred to here was the first of three vessels to carry that illustrious name. This one was a sidewheel, double-ended gunboat which had been launched on 30 Jan. 1862, and commissioned on 9 June 1862 at Baltimore, Cmdr. Charles Steedman in command. (Dept. of the Navy, *Dictionary of American Naval Fighting Ships*, G.P.O., Wash., D.C., 1970, p. 234.)

[12] Varnum's high ranking in his graduating class belies a high-spirited

I, Varnum

As I had a leave of absence until October 1st, 1872, I went to my old home in Massachusetts, as it was too hot to go to Florida. My home was then at Tallahassee where my father was Adjutant General of the State.[13]

I soon received my commission as 2d Lieutenant, 7th Cavalry, and orders to report to my Troop A, at Elizabethtown, Ky., Oct. 1st.[14] I spent a short time with my

---

youth capable of committing an act which could and did result in a court martial. Before a General Court Martial which convened at West Point, New York, 10 April 1871, pursuant to Special Orders No. 134, War Dept., Adj. Gen. Office, 4 April 1871, and to which Capt. J. S. Conrad, 2nd Inf. had been appointed President, Charles Varnum was arraigned and tried on the charge of "Sentinel deserting his post." Varnum pleaded "Not Guilty," particularly to the words, "did desert said post. . ." He was found guilty, however, and sentenced "To be confined in the area of the barracks until the ensuing encampment; to walk every Saturday afternoon of that time, equipped as a sentinel, from two (2) o'clock P.M. until ten (10) minutes before the first drum for parade, and to be confined to the chain of sentinels during the ensuing encampment." The sentence was approved by the Adj. Gen. except "to walk every Saturday afternoon of that time, etc." He explained the duty of the sentinel "is important and honorable, and by Army Regulations, all persons are required to observe respect toward sentinels. It is deemed improper to impose as punishment anything presenting the semblence of the performance of the duty of a sentinel." The remainder of the sentence was approved. (General Court Martial Orders No. 7, War Dept., Adj. Gen. Office, Wash., May 19, 1871.)

[13] In a personal letter to the editor from Col. Franklin M. Persons, Adj. Gen. of the State of Florida, dated 10 July 1981, he stated: "This Headquarters does not have any records for the particular period Varnum served as Adjutant General. His name is listed on our records as John Varnum, and he served as Adjutant General of Florida from 21 Feb. 1870 to 4 March 1877. In that this period is between the Civil War and the Spanish American War, information is very sparse. Units, biographies and rosters of personnel were scanned for John Varnum in each of the Civil and Spanish American War accounts, and no mention could be found."

[14] Troop A, 7th U. S. Cav., had been at Elizabethtown, Ky., since 3 April 1871, and changed stations to Louisville, Ky., on 8 March 1873, so Varnum was in this area for about six months only. Their primary activities were horse-buying, chasing the KKK, assuring voting rights to the previously disenfranchised and watching out for revenuers. "Troop" should be "company," as "troop" was not used until much later. We will use "troop" throughout to be consistent with Varnum.

uncles and cousins in Granville & Columbus, Ohio & then went to Louisville, Ky., and reported to my Colonel, S. D. Sturgis,[15] at Taylor Barracks,[16] and also where my Captain, M. Moylan,[17] who was at that time on recruiting service at Cincinnati, Ohio, and on Oct. 1st, I reported to my 1st Lieutenant [18] at Elizabethtown.

The troops, consisting of A, 7th Cavalry, and a company of the 4th Infantry, were quartered in houses in

---

[15] At that time. Col. Samuel D. Sturgis was serving actively in the capacity of Colonel and commanding 7th U. S. Cav. and of post of Louisville, Ky., from 29 March 1871 to 29 April 1873. (John M. Carroll, and Byron Price, *Roll Call On The Little Big Horn,* Ft. Collins, Co., 1974, p. 102.)

[16] Taylor Barracks was located in the southern outskirts of the city of Louisville, Ky., being bounded on the south by Ormsby Ave., east by First St., north by St. Catherine St., and west by Third St. Use of these barracks by the 7th Cav. was temporary, for from the date of its erection the station had been used successfully as a rendezvous for drafted men, a depot for deserters and a depot for the reception of troops to be mustered out of the service at the close of the Civil War. (John S. Billings, Surg. Gen. Rept., Circular No. 4, *A Report on Barracks and Hospitals With Descriptions of Military Posts,* War Dept., Wash., D.C., Aug. 17, 1871, p. 138.) That author goes on to state "Taylor Barracks consists of a series of poorly constructed wooden pavilions arranged in the form of a square . . . The walls of the buildings are battened, the roofs shingled, and, with the exception of the officers' quarters, the ceilings are opened." That report was made at the time of the occupation of the Barracks by the 7th Cavalry, and all things considered, the Barracks must have been a very uncomfortable place.

[17] Myles Moylan, born in Amesbury, Mass., on 17 Dec. 1838, was a soldier who had risen from the ranks. He began his military career as a Private in Co. E, 2nd Dragoons, on 8 June 1857. He joined the 7th Cav. on 28 July 1866. This recipient of the Medal of Honor (for Bear Paw Mountain on 30 Dec. 1877) received his Majority in the 10th U. S. Cav. on 8 April 1892, and retired almost to the day a month later. (Carroll and Price, pp. 146-47.) Because he had risen from the ranks he was often looked down upon by the other officers who had not seen enlisted service; however, Gen. Custer recognized in him the many attributes and qualities of a good soldier, and because of this paternalism was well treated by all most of the time.

[18] This would be 1st Lt. Algernon E. Smith of Newport, N.Y., who also had a beginning in the military within the enlisted ranks of the 7th U. S. Inf., Co. K, in June, 1862. He and Moylan must have enjoyed a close relationship considering their background. Smith, however, was killed at the Little Big Horn on 25 June 1876.

I, Varnum

town, and I lived at a small hotel.[19] General Custer was in command.

On the 25th of October I was ordered with twenty-five men to Huntsville, Alabama, for duty to assist the U. S. Marshal in serving warrants of arrest under the Reconstruction Laws.[20] I encamped near town. A few small detachments were sent out with deputies, but just before the election in Nov. we were all called for in small parties. I stored our baggage & left a corporal in charge and went with ten men to Fayetts Court House, Alabama, and was there on election day. The Marshal made several arrests assisted by the soldiers. Our appearance with warrants drove lots of voters to the swamps to hide, and apparently our move was for political purposes. We stayed in a small house and notes received by some of the prisoners looked suspicious.

[19] That would be the Brown-Pusey House, still standing today at 128 North Main St. in Elizabethtown. For more information on this building and this town, refer to the periodicals *Kentucky Progress Magazine,* Summer 1933; *In Kentucky,* vol. xx, #1, 1957, and the *Filson Club History Quarterly,* April 1938. Of more value, however, is the pamphlet printed especially for members of the Little Big Horn Associates attending the First Annual Convention, entitled *Custer's Kentucky: General George Armstrong Custer And Elizabethtown, Kentucky, 1871-1873,* by Lt. Col. (then Capt.) Theodore J. Crackel, later printed in the *Filson Club History Qtly.* in April 1974.

[20] There is and was no such thing as a body of "Reconstruction Laws" as referred to by Varnum. Instead, there were "Reconstruction policies." At this time there was no federal agency available to carry out the policies of the government, so it fell upon the soldiers, who were in the South in such numbers as to project a presence large enough to impose those federal policies. There was a Civil Rights Bill achieved by the Radicals over President Johnson's veto in April 1866. Sen. Lyman Trumbull felt the Freedman's Bureau should become the enforcement agency, but the May riot in Memphis created the need for more muscle, and the powers that be felt that strength should come from the War Department. It was then that the South was divided into five military districts and manned by the military, they to enforce civil rights. It was this assignment that Varnum found himself engaged in. For further reading on this subject see William S. McFeely, *Grant: A Biography,* N.Y., 1981.

I heard of a rescue. That night I gave orders in presence of the prisoners that in case of attack to rescue, the men should immediately kill the prisoners, and we would fight our way out or die trying. A prisoner asked to write a note & send it to his mother. I gave it, and sent the note. He assured me then that his friends had been warned and no rescue would be attempted.

We got away all right next day, but on the following day the Marshal took three men and made a detour through a place called Poplas Log Cove. He made two arrests of brothers, but in trying to join us he was fired into. One prisoner was killed; the other tried to escape, but was clubbed back onto his horse. One of my horses was killed, but my man mounted the dead prisoner's horse and left his with saddle, etc. They joined me all right.

The next day we arrived at Huntsville and the prisoners were placed in jail. I then went with my detachment to Thomas Barracks,[21] a small post, with our Company C of the 2d Infantry, Capt, W. F. Drum.[22]

I had to testify before a Congressional Committee sent there to investigate southern outrages, and on January 31st, I returned to Elizabethtown, Ky.

Soon after my return orders were received sending the 7th Cavalry to the Department of Dakota. My troops marched to Louisville, Ky., and after about a month's delay at Taylor Barracks, four troops, A, F,

---

21 This post was located about two miles northeast of the city of Huntsville, Al. The barracks consisted of only two framed buildings designed to quarter one company each. The post was put together in a very inferior manner and on insufficient foundations. (Billings, Circular No. 8, pp. 131-33.)

22 This would be William Findlay Drum of New York, a graduate of the U. S. Military Academy. His highest rank attained was brevet Lt. Col. He died 4 July 1892.

I, Varnum

H and I embarked by steamer for Cairo, Ill, where the rest of the regiment arrived from Memphis and New Orleans.

On the way up this river a prisoner charged with desertion, named Charles F. Smith,[23] and belonging to my troop, was being taken along. He was a magnificent physical specimen of manhood, handsome and powerfully built. A nine inch shell was attached to his leg & the shackle was riveted around his ankle. A considerable amount of liquor was obtained by the men on the dock while waiting to embark and after embarking, some disturbance took place on the hurricane deck. I was detailed as Officer of the Guard, and putting on my belt with my revolver, went up at once to investigate. The only light (it was after sunset) came from the flames coming from the smokestack. A fight was going on between some of the men near the rail, which was an iron rod about a foot high. I pushed my way to the center of the group when a blow from [one] of the contestants grazed my cheek. I used my revolver as a club and struck the man on the head with all my force. It knocked him over the rail and down about sixty feet into the Ohio river. I heard a chain run out over the iron rod & knew then that my man was the prisoner Smith. The river was out of its banks in the spring freshet & must have been more than a mile wide, perhaps two.

Man overboard was shouted & the steamer sounded

---

[23] This name is a mystery for there was no Charles Smith listed on the Muster Rolls at this time (1873), this from a letter from the National Archives to the editor, dated 20 July 1981. At about this time period, a Philip C. Smith, also of Co. A, deserted and was apprehended and escaped detention. The two stories sound very much alike, so perhaps Varnum confused the names.

to & search made, but the Captain said that if he had a nine inch iron shell attached to his leg he was past hope when he struck the waters. The boat went on its way. In the summer of '73, President Grant issued a proclamation of pardon to all deserters who surrendered before Dec. 1st (I think),[24] and served out their original enlistment. That winter Capt. Moylan received an official notice from the Commanding Officer at Jefferson Barracks, Mo.,[25] that Charles F. Smith, Troop A, 7th Cavalry, had surrendered as a deserter at that post and calling for his "Discriptive List" & papers in his case. At my request the Capt. asked that he be sent to the troop, but he was in trouble with the civil authorities in St. Louis and escaped & again deserted. I would much have liked to learn how he escaped from the river, but I was more than glad to learn that I had not been the cause of his death. I felt much relieved. My explanation is that he had already planned to escape & had cut the rivet that held his chains to his ankle. When he went into the water, the ball rolled *under* the rod, and the noise of the chains I heard was caused by this ball falling clear & pulling the chains back over the rod.

---

[24] That was General Orders No. 102, War Dept., Adj. Gen. Office, Wash., 10 Oct. 1873. It reads as follows: "The President of the United States commands it to be made known that all soldiers who have deserted their colors, and who shall on or before the first day of January, 1874, surrender themselves at any military station, shall receive a full pardon, only forfeiting the pay and allowances due them at the time of desertion; and shall be restored to duty without trial or punishment on condition that they faithfully serve through the terms of their enlistment."

[25] Jefferson Barracks, Mo., was established on 10 July 1826 on the west bank of the Mississippi River below St. Louis. First called Camp Adams, on 23 Oct. 1826, it was designated Jefferson Barracks. It was the starting point for numerous military and exploration expeditions. On 24 April 1871, Jefferson Barracks was turned over to the Ordnance Dept. and served as a recruiting station and for cavalry training. (Prucha, p. 81.) For a complete history see Billings, Circular No. 4, pp. 275-84.

I, Varnum

Being a powerful swimmer he, without the ball & chain, gained the shore.

The headquarters with the regimental staff of the 7th Cavy. was ordered to St. Paul, Minn. & Genl. Sturgis, with his adjutant & quartermaster departed for that place. Troops D & I under Major M. A. Reno, [26] were sent to Pembina, Dak. Terr.,[27] for duty on the northwestern boundary survey, and Genl. Custer (the Lt. Col.) with band and the remaining ten troops, went by rail to Yankton, Dak. Terr.[28]

The Territory at this time had about 20,000 population. There were a few small towns on the Missouri River above Yankton and within forty miles of that place. The only other town on the river was Bismarck,[29] then a small camp with one log house; the other building being merely framed tents. There was no population between the Missouri River and the Rocky Mountains and much was unexplored. A few troops were scattered along the river at Fort Randall,[30] Fort Sully,[31] the

[26] Maj. Marcus A. Reno was the senior Major of the 7th Cav. who was later to become the most controversial member of that famed regiment. During his time with the 7th he was to receive two courts-martial and ask for and receive one court of inquiry. He was finally dismissed from the Army on 1 April 1880, for "Conduct to the prejudice of good order and military discipline." He died 1 April 1889, at Wash., D.C., at age 54. (Carroll and Price, pp. 85-86.)

[27] Pembina, Dakota Terr., is located in northeast North Dakota, and was the site of the earliest trading post and center of white settlement in North Dakota (1797-98). (Webster's *Geographical Dictionary*, Springfield, Mass., 1966, p. 866.)

[28] Yankton, Dakota Terr., now South Dakota, was then the capital of Dakota Territory (1861-83). (Webster's, p. 1279.)

[29] First settled in 1871-72, and became Territorial Capital in 1883. (Webster's, p. 134.)

[30] Fort Randall, S.D., was established on 26 June 1856, on the right bank of the Missouri River as a base of operations and supplies for posts on the Upper Missouri and for protection of settlers against hostile Indians. (Prucha, p. 100. *See also* Billings, Circular No. 8, pp. 417-421, and Circular No. 4, pp. 386-87.)

Cheyenne Indian Agency [32] and Grand River Agency [33] for Sioux Indians, Fort Stevenson [34] and the Berthold Agency, [35] 75 to 100 miles above Bismarck, Fort Buford [36] at the mouth of the Yellowstone River, and one or two agencies between Buford and Fort Benton, [37] the head of navigation of the Missouri.

---

[31] Fort Sully, S.D., was established in Sept. 1863, as a result of the Sioux uprising and was first located on the east bank of the Missouri River about three miles below Pierre, S.D. This location was abandoned on 25 July 1866, when the garrison moved to a new site about twenty-five miles above Pierre. (Prucha, p. 110. *See also* Billings, Circular No. 4, pp. 388-90, and Circular No. 8, pp. 441-44.)

[32] The Cheyenne Indian Agency, S.D., was first designated Fort Bennett and was established on 17 May 1870 on the west bank of the Missouri River, seven miles above Fort Sully, for the purpose of controlling the Indians at the Cheyenne Agency. Until 30 Dec. 1878, it was designated the Post at Cheyenne Agency; then it was renamed Fort Bennett. This site is now inundated by Oahe Reservoir. (Prucha, pp. 60-61.)

[33] The proper designation for this was the Post at Grand River Agency, S.D. This post was established at the Agency, on the west bank of the Missouri, at the confluence of the Grand River in May, 1870. (Prucha, p. 76.)

[34] Fort Stevenson, N.D., was established on 22 June 1867, on the left bank of the Missouri River on a site now inundated by Garrison Reservoir. The post was part of the chain of military posts guarding the routes of travel to Montana. (Prucha, p. 109. *See also* Billings, Circular No. 4, pp. 394-99, and Circular No. 8, pp. 438-41.)

[35] Fort Berthold, N.D., was first a trading post and agency for Indians. In 1864 troops were sent to protect this trading post, located on the north bank of the Missouri River about thirty miles below the mouth of the Little Missouri, on a site now inundated by Garrison Reservoir. In 1865 a military post was established there. (Prucha, p. 61.)

[36] Fort Buford was established on 13 June 1866, on the left bank of the Missouri River near the mouth of the Yellowstone, as a part of a plan for a chain of military posts between Fort Leavenworth and the Columbia River. The post played an active part in settling Indian troubles and in establishing the Indians upon reservations. It was occupied continuously until its abandonment in 1895. (Prucha, p. 63. *See also* Billings, Circular No. 4, pp. 400-05, and Circular No. 8, pp. 399-402.)

[37] Fort Benton, on the left bank of the Missouri River at the head of navigation about 40 miles below the Great Falls of the Missouri, was occupied by U. S. troops on 17 Oct. 1869. Prior to that it had been a post of the American Fur Company, first called Fort Lewis and then named Fort Benton in honor of Sen. Thomas Hart Benton. (Prucha, p. 61. *See also* Billings, Circular No. 8, pp. 397-99, and Circular No. 4, pp. 405-06.)

I, Varnum

The Northern Pacific R. R. had built to Bismarck that year, and Fargo and Jamestown 200 & 100 miles east of Bismarck were small towns on that road. Nearly all the population was on the Minnesota border and near Yankton. We went into camp at Yankton and a terrible snow storm & blizzard drove us into town for shelter for ourselves & horses. I was sick, and with a few other officers stayed in camp though we feared all the time the tent would disappear with the gale. A warm wind soon melted the snow, and in May we started up the river marching 450 miles to Fort Rice [38] (now abandoned) where we arrived early in June 1873. This post was on the west bank of the Missouri river about thirty-five miles below Bismarck and was garrisoned by four companies of the 17th Infantry. Here a large force was being collected to escort the surveyors of the N.P.R.R. west to & up the Yellowstone River.

This force consisted of 20 companies of Infantry drawn from the 6th, 8th, 9th, 17th and 22d Regiments and our ten troops of cavalry under Custer, the whole commanded by Colonel D. S. Stanley [39] of the 22d.

---

[38] Fort Rice was established by Gen. Alfred Sully on 7 July 1864, as a supply base for his operations against the Sioux. It was located on the right bank of the Missouri River about ten miles north of the mouth of the Cannonball River. (Prucha, pp. 101-02. *See also* Billings, Circular No. 8, pp. 421-25, and Circular No. 4, pp. 390-94.)

[39] Col. David Sloan Stanley of Ohio, was a graduate of the U. S. Military Academy in 1848. He held many brevets for heroic service during the Civil War. (Heitman, Francis B. *Historical Register and Dictionary of the United States Army*, G.P.O., Wash., 1903, p. 915.) Because of Stanley's drinking problem and Custer's strong personality, there were bound to be many conflicts between the two on this expedition. (*See* Gen. George A. Custer, "Battling With The Sioux on the Yellowstone" in *Galaxy Magazine*, July 1876, pp. 91-102, also reprinted in *By Valor & Arms*, October 1974, pp. 4-19. *See also* Elizabeth Custer, *Boots and Saddles*, N.Y., 1885, pp. 271-312; and David S. Stanley, *Personal Memoirs of . . .* , Harvard Univ. Press, 1917, pp. 238-71.)

Generals Sheridan [40] and Terry [41] came to inspect us and give final instructions. The N. P. surveyors were under General Rosser,[42] a classmate of of Custer's at West Point and a famous Confederate Cavalry leader.

We left Fort Rice on June 20th, picked up the line of the survey on the Heart River west of Bismarck, and marched across the rolling prairies to the Yellowstone river on about the line of the present R. R. route. A stockade [43] was built at the river and supplies brought up by steamboats were unloaded, and leaving four

[40] Gen. Philip Henry Sheridan of Ohio who graduated from the U. S. Military Academy in 1848. He held the rank of Lt. Gen. from 4 March 1869 until retirement. He was Commander in Chief of the Army from 1 Nov. 1883 to 5 Aug. 1888. He died 5 Aug. 1888. (Heitman, p. 881.) For a full biography refer to his own *Personal Memoirs*, 2 vols., N.Y., 1888. He was to be Custer's champion throughout his entire military career.

[41] Gen. Alfred Howe Terry did not attend the U. S. Military Academy, but after a law degree from Yale, began a military career which saw many brevets. His highest rank held was Major General. (Heitman, p. 951.) It was after his death that the true relationship between Terry and Custer became common knowledge. One of the most important publications in that respect would be by Col. Robert P. Hughes (Terry's brother-in-law and aide-de-camp), "The Campaign Against The Sioux in 1876," which appeared in the *Journal of the Military Service Institute of the United States*, Jan., 1896, pp. 1-44. It stirred up a huge can of worms, especially the many attempts to charge Custer with disobedience of Terry's orders, the exact status of those written words being in great doubt and the subject of much controversy.

[42] Thomas L. Rosser of Texas resigned from the U. S. Military Academy on 22 April 1861, due to impending Civil War. He rose to the rank of Major General in the Confederate States of America forces by 1864. During the 1873 Northern Pacific Rail Road Expedition he was the Chief Engineer, and later held that position with the Canadian Pacific Rail Road (1881-86). (George W. Cullum, *1970 Memorial Edition of Register of Graduates and Former Cadets,* West Point Alumni Foundation, 1970, p. 255.) Custer's defeat of his old West Point friend at Toms Brook was to be a highlight in Custer's military career, though they remained the staunchest of friends afterwards, and Rosser was one of Custer's untiring champions after the former's death.

[43] This was variously known as Stanley's Stockade, Pease Fort, and presently Pease Bottom. It was the sight of one of the three engagements the 7th had with the Sioux on that expedition.

companies of Infantry and two troops of cavalry to guard them, we were ferried over to the north bank and continued the survey up that stream. The whole country abounded in antelope, and although they were shy, we killed a great many and had plenty of fresh meat.

We had a train of 280 six-mule teams besides ambulances and sutler's train of several wagons. Our steamboat came up above the mouth of Powder river after we left the stockade and delivered supplies of grain & rations, being the first boat above Buffalo Rapids.

One of the infantry companies had two 3″ ordnance guns. Our troop of Cavalry and our company of Infantry marched each day with the instrument men to protect them, and the other troops covered the supply train and scouted the country in advance.

On the night of August 3d, we camped on Sunday Creek about ten miles up from the Yellowstone. We had to pass through some very bad country and could not follow the Yellowstone itself. On the 4th, Custer took Troops A & B and went ahead to scout a trail for the wagons. We had about 100 men only. We crossed a high prairie covered with cactus, descended into a broad level valley of the Yellowstone, and marched up that a few miles and halted in a grove of cottonwood trees on the river bank to wait for the main command.

We unsaddled and picketed our horses in the grass, where there was good grass, and had eaten our lunch and I was about to take a nap with my Captain. We had two guards of a corporal & three men each posted on the outer edge of the herd and I was taking off my belt etc., when several shots were heard from the upstream flank of our bivouack. I ran in that direction at

once and joined the guard. Four or five Indians were
out on the prairie shooting at us from their ponies. To
Horse was sounded at once & while they were saddling
up Custer sent over a few more men to cover the command, and sent us our horses, saddled. We mounted &
the Indians retreated to a much larger bunch of trees,
but further up the stream. The men formed in columns
of fours, B Troop in advance and Custer headed out
onto the open plain and then parallel to it and about
200 yards off.

A few Indians continued to skirmish in front of us
and when we were opposite the timber, about 250 Indians in line, with war-bonnets and stripped almost
naked, rode up a bank out of the timber, yelling a war
cry. "To fight on foot – dismount – link horses," shouted
Capt. Moylan. I got busy forming a skirmish line. The
troop in front (B) under Lieut. Tom Custer,[44] covered
our front. Moylan handled the line and I had the left
facing the timber where the bulk of the Indians were.
We stood them off, but were getting short of ammunition, and I was ordered to advance, wheeling to my
right & get my left on the river.

The other troops were to fall back & I was to con-
form to the movement so as to get the troops into the
timber we had left, and under that cover to distribute
the ammunition in our saddle bags. This was carried
out, and then Custer took 20 men in column, gave me
20 in skirmish line, and Capt. Moylan with the balance
in reserve all mounted, charged the Indians. We ran
them for several miles and on our halting I saw columns

---

44 Tom Custer was the brother of Gen. Custer, and was to die with him
at the Little Big Horn. He also enjoyed the disinction of being one of the
very few men in history to be the recipient of two Medals of Honor.

of dust coming from the bluffs to our right. They proved to be six troops of Cavalry from the train, and soon afterwards Genl. Stanley arrived with the Infantry and train.[45]

When we got together Lieut. Hodgson,[46] who was 2d Lieut. of B Troop, & not yet been in a fight & who had that day been on duty with the guard at the train, was almost crying because he had missed the fight, and to me said, "Well, Varnum, what did you do?" "DO," said Genl. Custer, "he was the only officer that remained mounted through the fight. That is what he did."

I had often thought about what I would do in a fight when bullets were flying around me, and hoped I would have the nerve to do my duty. This compliment of the General's made my heart beat very fast. I felt I had been tried and not found wanting. The man who led my spare horse was shot through the arm.

The vetinary [sic] surgeon and a Mr. Baliran, civilian sutler, wandered away from the train searching for water, were killed, and a private of F Troop named Ball[47] was killed with the engineer's escort. His com-

---

[45] This entire episode is told in detail in Custer's report found in *Galaxy Magazine* and in *Boots and Saddles*. (See footnote 39.)

[46] Lt. Benjamin (Benny) Hodgson of Philadelphia graduated from the U. S. Military Academy in 1870, and was immediately assigned to the 7th U. S. Cav., and served with his command in South Carolina, Tennessee, Louisiana and on the 1873 Expedition on the Yellowstone and the 1874 Black Hills Expedition. He was killed at the Little Big Horn while attempting to cross the Little Big Horn River in the retreat. (Carroll and Price, p. 67.) Hodgson was one of the few young officers to enjoy a splendid relationship with all the officers of the 7th, except for a brief altercation with Lt. McIntosh. Evidently he was hard not to like, and this episode related here by Varnum may help explain in part his popularity with his peers.

[47] These were Veterinary Surgeon John Honsinger, Sutler Auguste Baliran, and Pvt. John Ball, Co. F of the 7th Cavalry. Pvt. Ball's body was not to be discovered until 4 Aug. He was at first listed as missing. These three men were alleged to have been killed by Rain-in-the-Face, who later boasted

panion put spurs to his horse and joined the train giving the alarm which brought 6 troops to and after the fight was over. The bodies of Dr. Honzinger & Mr. Baliran were brought to camp, but the body of Private Ball was not found till the return of the command. We wrapped the bodies of the two men in canvas and carried them to the next camp as we knew they would be dug up by the Indians to scalp them. Four cottonwood trees forming a small square were in our camp, and a grave was dug between them, and they were quietly buried after dark. The picket line of the band was streatched [sic] across the square and the horses stood over their graves all night completely obliterating all trace of the graves. A sketch of the ground was kept for future reference.

We soon found a large trail of Indians heading up the valley, and on the evening 5th of August, Custer, with eight troops of Cavalry, left the main command and followed it. We marched till about midnight and made a long march next day, and on the 7th, just below the mouth of the Big Horn river, the trail ended, the Indians having crossed the Yellowstone. We tried all the rest of the day to get across, but failed and bivouacked in the timber on the bank.

About daylight the next morning, August 8th, the Indians commenced firing across the river. They sent a party to swim the river below us and attract our attention and their main body of warriors crossed the Big Horn and then the Yellowstone above and came to the attack. A small party was sent down stream to

of the incident and was captured and jailed for the deed. Several men were wounded during this expedition, most notably Lt. Charles Braden. (*Returns of the Yellowstone Expedition*, Aug. 1873, signed by Gen. D. S. Stanley, Nat. Arch., Wash., D.C.)

watch the Indians in that direction, and our troops were assembled under the high bluffs that streatched from the Yellowstone back a short distance and then on down the river. I climbed this bluff in front of my troop and the Indians pressing in pretty fast, Custer ordered the troop dismounted and put in action to cover our position. As the men climbed the bluff, I forming them, Custer called to me to wheel it to the right across a ravine & drive the Indians out. This I did & was nicely remembered in Custer's report. See Appendix "Boots And Saddles" by Mrs. Custer. Lieut Charles Braden [48] was doing the same thing on our left and was shot through the thigh, breaking the bone badly.

When the Indians had arrived in our front, Custer charged with the remaining troops and drove the Indians away, but they escaped across the river. That P.M. Genl. Stanley arrived with the Infantry & train and the two pieces of artillery which opened fire on the Indians across the river driving them to the bluffs.

We had one man killed, Genl. Custer's orderly,[49] and several men wounded, but not seriously. Lieut. Braden, however, was in a serious condition. He was a large man weighing over 200 lbs. & his thigh bone shattered, and we had to march. An ambulance was taken apart and poles stretched from front to rear springs and a hand-litter suspended from them. He was then hauled by the

---

[48] Lt. Charles Braden of Michigan graduated from the U. S. Military Academy in 1869. He was breveted 1st Lieutenant on 27 Feb. 1890 for his action against the Indians on the Little Big Horn on 11 Aug. 1873, where he was severely wounded. He retired on 28 June 1878 because of these same wounds, which did not, however, prevent him from serving as an Instructor and Principal at the National Prep Academy for West Point at Highland Falls, N.Y. (Heitman, p. 237; Cullum, p. 264.)

[49] This would be Pvt. John H. Tuttle, Headquarters Company, who was killed on 11 Aug. near the mouth of the Big Horn River. (*Returns of Yellowstone Expedition.*)

men in rear of the wagon train, the litter being carried by hand over rough ground, and this for several hundred miles till at last he was sent down the river by steamboat. He never fully recovered from suffering & had to be retired from service.

We continued our march to Pompey's Pillar, a cut bluff on the Yellowstone. The Indians fired into our camp there, but no one was injured. The men were bathing in the river when fired into, so they were very fortunate.

We marched across to the Mussel Shell river & circled back to our old Stockade with no further serious incidents except that the Indians burned the grass and almost starved our horses which became so weak we had to walk & had therefore lost quite a number from exhaustion.

We then returned to the Missouri River to Fort Abraham Lincoln [50] after a campaign of about 1300 miles from Fort Rice & back. We spent the winter at Fort A. Lincoln, or 6 troops did and four went to Fort Rice 28 miles below.

John Smith, a sutler, had a herd of mules on the plains below the fort and sometime in the spring of 1874, Genl. Custer saw it being rapidly hurrying to the hills & being driven by only two or three men. Suspecting Indians, he sounded To Horse, and everyone ran for the stables. The six troops were soon mounted. He selected four best mounts from each troop and ordered

---

[50] Fort Abraham Lincoln in N.D., was built as a temporary camp on 14 June 1872, and named Fort McKeen. It was built on the west bank of the Missouri River near the present site of Bismarck, to protect the construction crews of the Northern Pacific Rail Road. On 15 Aug. 1872, the post was moved to a new site five miles away, and on 19 Nov. 1872, it was renamed Fort Abraham Lincoln. (Prucha, p. 55. *See also* Billings, Circular No. 8, pp. 392-94.)

me to command them and follow him taking as fast a gait as I thought I could keep up for a long ride. In about five miles we made them drop the herd and we skirmished with a few Indians and seriously wounded one who subsequently died in hospital at the Indian Agency at Standing Rock.[51]

We had the entire six troops on this trip as a support against any trap we might be drawn into, but my twenty-four men were the only ones who came in contact with the Indians.

The winter at Fort A. Lincoln was very dull. The weather was intensely cold going down in January to 50° below zero. Bismarck was five miles away and not one respectable woman in town. Prostitutes, gamblers & toughs of all kinds were in the majority and some business men. There was a post called Camp Hancock [52] in the town with our Co. of Infantry. Everybody drunk, and shooting of soldiers & gamblers were quite frequent.

The failure of J. Cooke [53] put an end to the N. P. construction for several years. The R. R. did not run trains after Nov 1st, and not until about April 1st. It was too cold to drill and our only duty was routine

---

[51] Standing Rock Agency, was at Fort Yates, N.D. This post was established on 23 Dec. 1874, at the already existing Agency, on the Missouri River, to aid in the control of Indians established on reservations on the Missouri River. This post was designated Fort Yates on 30 Dec. 1878. (Prucha, p. 118.)

[52] Camp Hancock, N.D., was established on 9 Aug. 1872, on the east bank of the Missouri River, at Bismarck, where the Northern Pacific Rail Road crosses the river. (Prucha, p. 77. *See also* Billings, Circular No. 8, pp. 409-10.)

[53] This is Jay Cooke, an American banker (1821-1905). His company marketed government bonds for financing the Civil War. During the Civil War he was a fiscal agent for the U. S. Treasury (1862-64, 1865). After the war he financed construction of western railroads, especially the Northern Pacific Rail Road. This effort failed, putting a quick end to that expedition in 1873 and the expansion of the rail line. It also precipitated a financial panic. (Webster's, *Biographical Dictionary,* Springfield, Mass., 1966, p. 346.)

guard. But we were comfortable and the officers and their wives gave very pleasant entertainments.

In 1874, an expedition for the exploration of the Black Hills was planned, and July 4th,[54] I think, the troops of the 7th Cavalry with Capt. Lloyd Wheaton,[55] C. O. of the 20th & Capt. L. H. Sanger,[56] C. O. of the 17th Infty., and a large train left the post with supplies for sixty days. We marched west to the Little Missouri river & south to the Belle Fourche, then entered the hills near Inyan Kara peak, and passed through the hills emerging near where Rapid City, S. D., now is. We had our officers of the Engineer Corps (Capt. Ludlow)[57] & assistants who mapped the country. Also a corps of scientists & a photographer.[58] Two practical miners went along hunting for gold & on whose reports the hills were invaded the following year by hundreds of miners. We were gone sixty days & marched about 1200 miles in all.

After our return I applied for a leave of absence for six months to visit my home in Florida. But just before my departure in Oct. orders were received to send six

54 July 2, 1874.

55 Lloyd Wheaton of Illinois first entered service as a 1st Sergeant of Co. E, 8th Illinois Inf., on 20 April 1861. By July he had been commissioned a 1st Lieutenant. His highest brevet rank was Major General of Volunteers. He was also the recipient of the Medal of Honor. (Heitman, p. 1023.)

56 This was Louis H. Sanger of Maine who began his military career as a Private of Co. C., 1st Battalion, 17th Inf. on 19 Sept. 1861. He was commissioned in July 1862. He was in the 1876 Sioux Campaign commanding Co. G, 17th Inf., Dakota Column. (Heitman, p. 859, and Carroll & Price, p. 154.)

57 William Ludlow of New York was a graduate of the U. S. Military Academy in 1864 in the discipline of engineering. Before the end of the Civil War he had received promotions to include brevet Major General. (Heitman, p. 646.)

58 It is to this photographer, William H. Illingworth, that we owe so much for his keen skill in photographing this expedition.

troops of the regiment to New Orleans on account of political troubles there. I gave up my leave to go with my troop. We worked all night and Troops A & E left the next morning from Bismarck and went by train to Chicago and thence to New Orleans. Orders there sent A Troop to Livingston, Ala., and E Troop to Selma, Ala.[59] We remained in the cars all night and left for Mobile next day. Thence to Meridian, Miss. We took this last trip as the tail end of a long train of empty freight cars.

On a long hill we had to stop repeatedly as the engine could not haul us, and then it would start with an awful jerk. I was up about the train lots at night, and after a sudden jerk we started back & commenced going faster rapidly. I had an inspiration that the train had broken in two & rushed into the men's car & woke the men and rushed them to the brakes. We were then going furiously down hill. We managed to stop the train and I sent one of my men back with a lantern in time to stop a passenger train behind us. The head of our train went on to a siding and then the engine came back after us.

We left Meridian next day & went to York, Ala., and took the Ala. & Chattanooga north. We had two baggage cars, four stock cars and two coaches. This R. R. was bankrupt & in hands of a receiver & in awful shape. It was only ten miles to Livingston. About three miles out one of the stock cars went off the track. We were running slow, it being the car next to the baggage. Capt. Moylan left me with part of the men and took the rest on the forward cars & he & his wife on the engine went on to Livingston. This was about 11 P.M.

---

[59] They departed Bismarck on 29 Sept. 1874 for the Department of the Gulf, and then departed there for Dakota Terr. on 18 May 1875.

Early in the morning a wrecking train came and cut open the end of the stock car and got my horses out and we mounted up bareback with our arms etc., and finished our journey.

There was a company of Infantry encamped in the court house square. We went into camp just outside the town limits – on the Sucarnoochee River. The Infantry soon left. Capt. Moylan was soon ordered away on a horse purchasing board & I was left alone with the troops. I got authority to hire an old hotel with stables for the troop in town and we were very comfortable. We had little to do with political troubles except to furnish guards in small parties for U. S. Marshals making arrests.

I was again investigated by a Congressional Sub-Committee, but had nothing to tell.

I had a month's leave of absence in February, 1875, when the Capt. returned, and visited by home in Tallahassee, and about May 1st, we were ordered back to Dakota. We went up the Mobile & Ohio to Corinth, thence to Cairo & by Ill. Central to Yankton & marched sixty miles to Fort Randall. Troops E & H joined us and we were held that summer on the road to Red Cloud Agency [60] trying to keep intruders out of the Black Hills country until a treaty could be arranged with the Sioux Indians. [61] A big council was to take

---

[60] Fort Robinson (First called Camp Robinson) was established on 8 March 1874. It was built on the left bank of the White River in northwestern Nebraska at the Red Cloud Agency near present day Crawford, Nb., to maintain order among the Sioux warriors settled there. It was an important base of operations against the Indians. (Prucha, p. 102. *See also* Billings, Circular No. 8, pp. 366-67.)

[61] Often, detractors of the military presence out west will suggest little or no effort was made to keep prospectors out of the Black Hills; it was they who broke the Laramie Treaty of 1868. This is patently untrue. That treaty,

I, Varnum

place on Chadron Creek in Neb. that summer and delegations from all the tribes assembled there. It came near ending in an outbreak and massacre of the Commissioners, but finally ended in the cession of all lands between the Belle Fourche (or North. Cheyennes) and south fork Cheyenne River & fixing the western boundary of the Sioux Reservation on the 103d meridian longitude. This last was important as no definite boundary on the west had heretofore been fixed and Sioux and Crows both claimed the country and were hostile to each other.

My troop was sent west to the White River about 150 miles from Fort Randall, and I made two trips to Wounded Knee Creek about 75 miles further, but everything was quiet at this time. In September we returned to Fort Randall and marched up the Missouri to Ft. A. Lincoln, making a summer's work for me of over 1000 miles campaigning.

I then applied for five months leave of absence. My Capt. disapproved because he would be alone with the troop, his 1st Lieut. being on other duty. My application had hardly left when orders came for two troops

---

by the way, was FIRST broken by the Sioux when they violated the clause which permitted the railroad surveyors to survey through their land by killing the men of the Yellowstone Expedition and engaging in three combative efforts with the 7th Cav. A little known Proclamation by Brig. Gen. George Crook, dated Camp Crook, D. T., 29 July 1875, specifically directed miners "or other unauthorized citizens" out of the "Indian Reservation of the Black Hills" until "some new treaty arrangements have been made with the Indians." It went on to say that he, Gen. Crook, was authorized to remove all interlopers. All were advised to "leave the territory known as the Black Hills, the Powder River, and Big Horn country by and before the 15th day of August next." It is interesting to note that General Crook used the words "Indian Reservation of the Black Hills." All efforts were made to protect the rights of the Indians, but the lure and greed for gold was bigger than the Army. Another interesting point is the interpretaion of the broken Laramie Treaty of 1868 which provided the Indians with the Black Hills. All interpretations involving the Black Hills are quite sensitive and open to controversy.

of Cavy. and one of Infantry to go to Fort Stevenson 75 miles away, as the Sioux were threatening the Ree Indian Agency at Fort Berthold. Troops A & D & Co. B, 6th Infty. were ordered to go. There were no officers with D at this time so I was ordered to Command D. Capt. Weir [62] of that troop joined on the road, however.

On arrival we found there was no trouble & A Troop & Co. B were ordered back, but I was held by Capt. Weir with Troop D. We got back to Fort A. Lincoln, however, on the 30th or 31st of October. It had been very cold weather & we were glad to get to our fires again. Here my application for leave of absence was returned to me disapproved "as my services could not be spared on account of Indian troubles on the upper river," or words to that effect. Capt. Weir had telegraphed on return from Bismarck, and that same day I was given a telegram authorizing me to "take advantage of the leave of absence applied for by me."

The N.P.R.R. was to run a train east the following day & take out the water pipes at the water tanks & it would be the last train till spring. I packed up & left on it. At Dept. Headquarters the Adj. Genl. had made a mistake in some way, but I was in St. Paul. No way to get back and no leave of absence. Genl. Terry told me to make a new application for what I wanted & told the Adj. Genl. to issue the orders. I applied for six months & got it.

---

[62] Capt. Thomas Bell Weir was a graduate of the Univ. of Michigan in 1861, two months later joining Co. B, 3rd Michigan Cavalry. He was breveted Lieutenant Colonel during the Civil War. He joined the 7th Cav. on 28 July 1866, the date the regiment was organized. During the Little Big Horn fight he commanded Co. D in the hilltop fight. After the battle he was detailed on cavalry recruiting service in New York City and because of a deteriorating health problem, suddenly died on 9 Dec. 1876. (Ken Hammer, *Biographies of the 7th Cavalry*, Ft. Collins, Co., 1972, p. 91.)

I, Varnum

I went to my old home in Dracut, Mass. and spent some time stopping en-route to visit my Ohio cousins, and then in Washington & went to Tallahassee, Fla. to visit my parents. My father was Adjutant General of the State. He was building a state agricultural college at Eau-Gallie on Indian River,[63] and was going there later, so I left him and went up the St. Johns river to visit some more cousins at Fort Gates [64] above Palatka and finally joined my father & went up Eau-Gallie. We got back to Tallahassee in March, and I got a telegram from Genl. Custer that my regiment was to take the field with a large expedition against hostile Indians.

I also got a letter from Washington informing me that it had been requested that I be ordered to join. It did not *order* me to join however, so I had to pay my own travel expenses. I went back, however, and reported to Genl. Terry in St. Paul.[65] I was placed on duty there and ordered back to my post.

Here Major Reno was in command in absence of Genl. Custer in Washington,[66] but he left orders that I be ordered to organize and command the Indian Scouts on the campaign. I enlisted about 60 Ree Indians

[63] The State Agricultural College had been approved for construction at Eau-Gallie by the Board of Trustees on 1 May 1875. By 7 March 1877, however, an act was approved to move the college to a more central location, Lake City, near Gainesville. It is now consolidated with the Univ. of Florida in Gainesville.

[64] Fort Gates was built at an undetermined date, but was one of the many forts established in Florida as a result of the Seminole Wars of 1836-43 and 1855-56. (Prucha, p. 139.)

[65] Whenever speaking of reporting to St. Paul, it is likely the soldier is reporting to Fort Snelling, a fort established in 1819. This was Gen. Terry's Headquarters, and also headquarters for the Department of the Dakota. An excellent reference is *Old Fort Snelling, 1819-1858* by Marcus L. Hansen, published by the State Hist. Soc. of Iowa in 1918.

[66] Gen. Custer had been subpoenaed to appear before the Clymer Committee investigating the Belknap scandal.

including the half-breeds. Fred Gerard [67] was employed as Ree Interpreter, and a negro, Isaiah,[68] as Sioux Interpreter. Charlie Reynolds [69] and a Ree Indian, Bloody Knife,[70] were employed as guides and attached to my detachment. I had one soldier as a sort of personal orderly.

The expedition organized in camp below the fort, the entire 7th Cavalry and parts of the 6th & 17th Infantry and a large wagon train. General A. H. Terry commanded. Custer commanded the 7th Cavalry. Major M. A. Reno was the only other cavalry field officer. The Adjt., Lieut. Cooke,[71] and Q. M. Nowlan [72]

---

[67] Frederick F. Gerard had been hired on as an interpreter for the Arikara and Sioux Indian Scouts. Years later after the Little Big Horn he opened a store in Mandan (1883); moved to Minneapolis in 1890 and was employed by the Pillsbury Mills as an advertising agent. He died on 13 Jan. 1913 at St. Cloud. (Hammer, p. 20.)

[68] Isaiah Dorman was hired on as Interpreter. He had formerly been a slave, a woodcutter for Durfee & Peck, and was now married to a Santee Sioux woman. He was killed at the Little Big Horn. (Hammer, p. 19.)

[69] Charles Alexander Reynolds was hired on as a guide. He was born in Illinois on 20 March 1842. He tried unsuccessfully a career as a trader. He became successful as a buffalo hunter and guide. (Hammer, p. 22.) For additional reading see John M. Carroll (ed.), *Charley Reynolds: Soldier, Hunter, Scout and Guide,* Bryan, Tx., 1978.

[70] Bloody Knife was reputedly Custer's favorite scout. He was an Arikara-Sioux, and had long been employed in government service. He was killed at the Little Big Horn. (Hammer, pp. 17-18.) For additional reading see Ben Innis, *Bloody Knife!,* Ft. Collins, Co., 1973.

[71] William Winer Cooke had been assigned Adjutant of the 7th Cav., the Dakota Column. He had been born in Canada on 29 May 1846. His first experience in the military was an appointment as 2nd Lieutenant, 24th New York Cav., on 26 Jan. 1864. His highest brevet rank was Lieutenant Colonel. He was killed at Little Big Horn at the age of 29. (Carroll and Price, p. 123.)

[72] Henry James Nowlan was the Regimental Quartermaster of the 7th Cav. He had been born on the Island of Corfu on 18 June 1837. He was first commissioned a 1st Lieutenant in the New York Cav. on 17 Jan. 1863. After service in the Civil War and under Custer at Washita in 1868 and other campaigns, he survived the Little Big Horn, was breveted Major on 27 Feb. 1890, and died at Hot Springs, Ar. on 10 Nov. 1898. (Carroll and Price, pp. 148-49.)

were with Headquarters. Capt. E. W. Smith [73] was
Actg. Adj. Genl. Capt. R. P. Hughes [74] & 1st Lieut.
E. B. Gibbs [75] were A.D.C. Capt. O. E. Michaelis,[76]
Ord. Off., & 1st Lieut. Edwd. Maguire,[77] engineer
officer.

We marched west by the old Stanley trail & turning
south struck Powder River about twenty miles above
its mouth. Major Reno, with six troops, was detached
from here to scout to the forks of the Little Powder
river – to join us on the Yellowstone near the mouth
of Tongue River. We then marched Powder river to
the mouth. Here we met steamboats with supplies, and
dropped our train, leaving Infantry to guard it.

We took mules from the train and pack saddles, or
aparajos rather, and marched up the south bank of

---

[73] Edward Worthington Smith was Captain in the 18th Inf., the Dakota
Column. He was born in Vermont on 16 Dec. 1832, and first saw service as
a 1st Lieutenant on 14 May 1861. He had highest brevet rank of Lieutenant
Colonel. (Carroll and Price, pp. 156-57.)

[74] Robert Patterson Hughes was Captain in 3rd Inf., Dakota Column, aide-
de-camp and brother-in-law to Gen. Terry. He was born in Pennsylvania
on 11 April 1839. He first saw service as an enlisted man in Company E of
the 85th Pennsylvania Volunteers on 25 April 1861, but by 11 Oct. he had
been commissioned a 1st Lieutenant. His highest rank was Major General on
1 April 1902, ten days before he retired. (Carroll and Price, p. 134.)

[75] Eugene Beauharnais Gibbs was 1st Lieutenant of the 6th Inf., also aide-
de-camp to Gen. Terry. He had been born on 19 May 1832 in Rhode Island.
His first service was as a 2nd Lieutenant of the 2nd California Volunteers
on 17 Sept. 1871. Highest rank he attained was Captain. (Carroll and Price,
pp. 129-30.)

[76] Otho Ernest Michaelis was the Ordnance officer of the Dakota Column.
He had been born in Germany on 3 Aug. 1843, enlisted as a Private in the
23rd Regiment of the National Guard, State of N.Y., in June 1863. Highest
rank he attained was Major. (Carroll and Price, p. 143.)

[77] Edward Maguire was the Engineer officer for the Dakota Column. He
had been born in Tennessee on 31 Aug. 1847. He attended the U. S. Military
Academy and graduated in 1867. He was ordered immediately to the Corps
of Engineers. He survived the Little Big Horn and continued a distinguished
career in the Army as an Engineer, but attained only the rank of Captain.
(Carroll and Price, pp. 74-75.)

the Yellowstone to Tongue river where Major Reno rejoined us. He reported he had struck a big Indian trail going up the Rosebud.

Keeping a steamboat with us, we marched to the mouth of the Rosebud and made a junction with Col. John Gibbon [78] with six companies of the 7th Infantry & four troops of the 2d Cavalry, from the Montana forts, who had marched down the Yellowstone from Fort Ellis.[79]

I do not care to write any history of the Custer massacre [80] and shall confine myself to my own personal experience. General Custer, with the entire regiment and my scouts, left the mouth of the Rosebud on June 22, 1876. I had only 24 of my scouts which included three half-breeds, two Jackson bros.[81] and Billy Cross.[82] My two interpreters & Charlie Reynolds & Bloody Knife, guides. The remainder of my scouts had been

---

[78] John Gibbon was commanding the 7th Inf., Montana Column. He had been born in Pennsylvania on 20 April 1827, and graduated from the U. S. Military Academy in 1847. He served in the War with Mexico (1847-48), against the Seminoles (1849-50), and of course the Civil War, rising to the rank of Brevet Major General. (Carroll and Price, pp. 59-61.)

[79] Fort Ellis, Mt., was established on the left bank of the East Gallatin River east of the present city of Bozeman, Mt., on 27 Aug. 1867, for protection against Indians. It was abandoned on 31 Aug. 1886. (Prucha, p. 73. See also Billings, Circular No. 4, pp. 406-08 and Circular No. 8, pp. 404-08.)

[80] Any number of good references can be read to satisfy the student, but highest on the editor's personal list are two books, Ken Hammer, *Custer In 76*, Provo, Ut., 1976, and Dr. John S. Gray, *Centennial Campaign*, Ft. Collins, Co., 1976. There are any number of other good references, but for sheer pleasurable reading of scholarly works, these are the best.

[81] These would be William Jackson, born in Fort Benton in 1856, a quarter Pikuni Blackfoot Indian scout, and Robert Jackson, born at Fort Benton in 1854, who also served on the 1873 and 1874 expeditions. (Hammer, p. 35.)

[82] Billy Cross was a part blood Dakota Indian scout who was serving his third enlistment at the time of the Little Big Horn. He was listed as missing in action on the muster rolls, but was not killed. He lived for some years after that, and as early as 4 July 1876, he gave his story to a news correspondent of *Chicago Tribune*. (Hammer, p. 32.)

sent away from time to time with mail or dispatches. I also had our guide, Herendine,[83] a white man from Gibbon's command. I do not know the correct spelling of his name. And six Crow scouts from the same source.

These Crows were in their own country and knew it thoroughly. They were at war with the Sioux and were actually trying to steal their ponies, or cut off any stragglers. Mich Boyer,[84] a half-breed, was interpreter for the Crows.

We marched about twenty miles the first day & the following day were on a heavy trail leading up the valley. The whole valley had evidently been a camp during the spring, and buffalo had been there, and the Indians had been drying meat.

My duty was to cover the front of the command with scouts and to see that no trail led *out* of the one we were following. This necessitated my riding a good many miles more than the main command, in my work. Early in the P.M. of the 24th, I was sent for by the Genl. who said that Lieut. Godfrey[85] had reported that a large trail had left the valley about ten miles back and

[83] This is George B. Herendeen, scout, born at Parkman, Oh., on 28 Nov. 1846. He joined Custer's campaign on 22 June 1876. He survived the Little Big Horn and was later engaged in the Nez Perce Campaign. He testified at the Reno Court of Inquiry in 1879. (Hammer, p. 20.)

[84] This is Mitch Bouyer who was killed with the Custer column at Little Big Horn. He was part blood Sioux. (Hammer, p. 18.)

[85] Edward Settle Godfrey, Co. K, 7th Cav., Dakota Column, was born in Ohio on 9 Oct. 1843. His military career began as an enlisted man in Co. D, 21st Ohio Inf. From there he attended the U. S. Military Academy, graduating in 1867. He served with Custer at the Washita, and the Yellowstone, Black Hills and Sioux expeditions. He was on the scout under Benteen and later at Reno Hill at the Little Big Horn. He was the recipient of a Medal of Honor for gallantry for action in the Nez Perce Campaign. Later served in the 1st, 9th and 12th Cav. Regiments. He retired as a Brigadier General on 9 Oct. 1907. (Carroll and Price, pp. 61-63.) He was probably the most vocal supporter of Custer and his actions at the Little Big Horn.

led east. I said I did not believe it, but he sent me back to investigate. Taking some scouts & changing my horse, I went for an extra twenty miles for nothing.

A small branch stream had steep banks and the Indians' travois had gone up the stream to get a crossing & then returned to the Rosebud valley.

The main command made about twenty miles that day. We were getting supper in my camp when the General sent for me. He said that the Crows believed we would find the Indians in the Little Big Horn valley. That in the divide between the Rosebud and that stream was a "Crow Nest," a big hollow, where the Crows used to go and hide when on horse-stealing expeditions against the Sioux. That from there they could see in the early morning when the camp fires started, and tell whether they were there or not, and estimated their strength. Custer said he wanted an intelligent white man to go with them and get what information he could from them & send him a message with that information. I said, "That means me." He said he did not like to order me on such a trip and that I had already had a hard day of it. I said he made me Chief of Scouts, and I objected to his sending anyone else unless he had lost faith in me. He said he thought that was about what I would say, and for me to go. He said I was to leave about 9 o'clock and get there before daylight. I would take the Crows & interpreters and I said I wanted one white man to talk to and asked for Charlie Reynolds, which he approved.

He said he would start at 11 o'clock and be at the base of the divide before morning & he thought I could locate him from the bluffs where I would be. Having ridden over 50 miles, I started at 9 P.M. for a ride of 20 more with only Indians & one white man. I took about a dozen Ree scouts for messengers. I arrived at the "Crow Nest" about 2 A.M. It was a disagreeable ride, in single file, keeping near the brush and a small tributary to the Rosebud, and the feeling that the one white man with me was the only person I could depend upon in case of trouble, as the Indians would all scatter on their own account in case we were attacked, made me feel I was not in the safest kind of an expedition.

We lay down till daylight began to appear and then climbed the steep slopes to the crest of the hill, leaving our horses with the Ree scouts in the Nest. The Crows said there was a large village in the Little Big Horn Valley, and pointed to the big pony herd. I could not see it. They said: "No look for horses, look for worms." But I could see neither: I could see on a branch between me and the river one teepee standing and one partly wrecked. They proved to be full of dead bodies from the fight of Genl. Crook [86] of June 17th of which of course we were ignorant at that time.

---

[86] Brig. Gen. George Crook was commanding the column from the Dept. of the Platte. He was born in Ohio on 23 Sept. 1829, and graduated from the U. S. Military Academy in 1852, and first served on frontier duty in California where he was wounded with an arrow in a skirmish on 2 July 1857. Later he served in the Civil War with distinction and was breveted a Major General. He then served in various campaigns and expeditions, most notably against the Snake Indians in 1867, the Piutes in 1868, and was then in command of the Dept. of Arizona. He was later sent to the Dept. of the Platte where he was at the time of the Sioux Expedition of 1876. His column was to march from present day Sheridan, Wy., up Rosebud Valley and join with Custer's and Gibbon's columns. However, on 17 June 1876, in the Rosebud Valley, he had a minor engagement against Crazy Horse and some of his warriors, with Crook getting the worst of it. He retreated to point of origin, and then went hunting for gold, game and then fishing in the Big Horn Mountains *without ever sending word to either Gibbon or Custer he was leaving the field of operations.* This decision allowed the Sioux to escape from the Little Big Horn, the exact thing Terry wanted to prevent. Crook later was engaged in the Apache Wars in Arizona in the 1880's, allowing

I sent back some Ree scouts with a note to the General reporting what the Crows said they saw. I could see smoke coming from a ravine several miles away where Custer was evidently camped, and later saw the dust of his column approaching.

While on the hill we saw an Indian riding a pony and leading another on a long lariat, and a boy behind, also mounted. They were in front of us, a mile or so off, riding parallel to the ridge but evidently heading for a gap to our right where the trail crossed the divide. Reynolds, myself, Mich Boyer, and two Crows started to intercept them and kill them so they would not discover the approach of Custer. The country was very broken, and we had not gone far before we were called back by the Crows on the hill. They said the Indians had changed their course. But they changed it again and did cross on the trail, and we watched them discover our column, when they disappeared.

Later, on a divide parallel to the stream up which Custer was approaching, I saw seven Indians in single file riding toward the Rosebud. From where we were they were outlined against the sky and looked like giants on immense horses. Suddenly they disappeared behind the crest, but black spots reappeared showing they were on the watch. They had evidently seen Custer's column.

The column arrived at the trail-crossing of the divide about 10 A.M., and Custer came at once to where I was, I riding out to meet him. We climbed the bluff and the Indians tried to show Custer what they saw. But he said he believed he had excellent eye sight but could see nothing.

Lt. Gatewood to talk Geronimo into surrender, but himself losing the Apaches on their way back to his military post. The editor believes him to be the most over-rated officer in the U. S. Army, and one who deserved censure for his retreat in 1876.

I, Varnum

Mich Boyer then said, "If you don't find more Indians in that valley than you ever saw together before, you can hang me." "It would do a damned sight of good to hang you, wouldn't it?" replied Custer. And we went down the hill and took four horses and rejoined the troop.

Custer called the officers together, but I did not attend as I had had nothing to eat or drink that day, so I searched the haversacks & canteens of my friends. The command mounted up & I reported for orders. Custer asked if I felt able to continue scouting. I said I had to ride anyway, & one place was as good as another. He said go ahead then. Lieut. Hare [87] reported to me the night before for duty and I sent him to the right front and I took the left front of the advance. From every hill where I could see the valley I saw Indians mounted.

We marched down a small tributary of the Little Big Horn River. I reported my observations several times. The valley of the river on the left bank is broad and level, but steep and sometimes almost perpendicular bluffs under the right bank from which we were approaching. Behind the highest part of the bluff was the main Indian village. The small branch down which we were advancing empties into it about two miles above the village.

The last time I reported, probably two miles from the river, I saw squadron of 3 troops passing the head of the column at a trot. I asked where they were going & the Genl. said, "To begin the attack." I asked in-

[87] Luther Hare of Texas graduated from the U. S. Military Academy in 1874, and was with Co. K of the 7th Cav, at the Little Big Horn. He commanded the Indian scouts. He survived the Little Big Horn and was later engaged in the Nez Perce Campaign of 1877. He was in the field against the Sioux in 1890. (Carroll and Price, pp. 63-64.)

struction & he said to go on with them if you want to. Lt. Hare & I and my whole party started at the trot. Lieut. Geo. D. Wallace,[88] a classmate of mine & dear friend & old roommate, was riding at the head of the column with the Genl. He was acting topographical officer. I called back to him, "Come on Nick, with the fighting men. I don't stay back with the coffee coolers." Custer laughed and waved his hat and told Wallace he could go & Wallace joined me.

It so happened that his Troop G & my A were with the advancing squadron under Major Reno. We put spurs to our horses and crossed the river with the command and then pulled out ahead, with the scouts, guides, etc. The valley was full of Indians riding madly in every direction. We advanced rapidly down the valley, the Indians retiring before us for about a mile, Wallace, Hare & myself riding together.

Suddenly the Indians began advancing towards us & looking back I saw that the troops were dismounting to fight on foot. My scouts had disappeared. We rode back to the line of troops which rested its right on the timber which bordered the stream. Across the timber, on the other side of the stream, was a high bluff & looking up I saw the gray horse Troop E in column. So I knew that some troops were passing to the other end of the village via the bluffs. There were plenty of Indians and the fight waxed hot. We had about 120 men total.

Capt. Moylan said that the Indians in our rear were

---

[88] George Daniel Wallace, Co. G, 7th Cav., was born 29 June 1849, in South Carolina. He graduated from the U. S. Military Academy in 1872, just in time to serve with the 7th Cav. in South Carolina and Tennessee, the Yellowstone, Black Hills and Sioux campaigns of 1876. He survived the Little Big Horn only to lose his life at the Battle of Wounded Knee on 29 Dec. 1890, at the age of 41. (Carroll and Price, pp. 111-12.)

getting to the horses, and I rode back & put them in the woods, and coming out of the woods I saw Reno with G Troop going through the woods to attack the village. He told me to go to Moylan's line and see what was going on & let him know. I met Lt. Hodgson, his adjutant, who said his horse was wounded, he thought. He was joining Reno and I told him to report what the status of affairs was on Moylan's line, and rode to the edge of the timber. There was a cut bank surrounding the timber & the men were behind it. Moylan told me he was getting out of ammunition & I brought the horses up in the timber in rear of the line so the men could get the extra ammunition from their saddle bags. Then I dismounted and tied my horse to a tree and went to the river.

I met Charlie Reynolds & Fred Gerard, the interpreter, and asked how things were going. They said things looked mighty bad. Fred Gerard had a half-pint flask of whiskey & said, "Let's take a drink. It may be our last." It was the last for poor Charlie Reynolds.

Just then I heard a commotion in the woods and heard men saying, "We are going to charge." I ran to my horse & mounted, but the men crowded me into a little path & it was some time before I could get out. When I got on the plain the column was racing for the bluffs. A heavy column in front – about eight or ten feet – and from there back for two or three hundred yards the men were scattered in twos & single file & the Indians surrounding on the flank with their Winchesters laying across their saddles and pumping them into us. There was a long gap for me to ride to catch up and I had a thoroughbred horse under me. I soon made it & fortunately without being hit. I was soon at the head of the column and tried to check it saying we could not run away from Indians. We must get down & fight.

Maj. Reno was there, however, & informed me that he was in command. I subsided. We soon struck the river & nearly all the Indians left us. Lieut. Hodgson received a bullet while crossing and was killed. My orderly Pvt. Strode,[89] had been shot through the thigh & his horse was falling. I dismounted and caught an M Troop horse, and with the aid of a sergt. of A Troop we put Strode on it.

Meanwhile the command was climbing the steep bluff on a "hog back" slope. I started up another when I heard men calling me back. I did not know why at this time, but came back & went up with the column.

I saw Dr. De Wolf [90] going up where I did with his orderly. Men were calling to him. He turned & just then received a bullet which killed him when about half way up the bluff. Our men had seen a few Indians laying for persons going that way & that is why I was called back.

We arrived at this crest and the Indians had left us. We had a number of wounded, some of them very

[89] Pvt. Elijah T. Strode was wounded in the right ankle in the valley fight. He was born in Monroe County, Ky. and enlisted in the 7th Cav. in 1872 in Elizabethtown, Ky. He was discharged 24 June 1877, but re-enlisted and promoted to Sergeant in Co. D in that same year. During the Nez Perce Campaign he was once again wounded at the Snake Creek fight. He was murdered on 14 Feb. 1881 at Fort Yates, Dakota Terr. (Hammer, p. 55.)

[90] James Madison De Wolf was a contract surgeon with the 7th Cav., holding no rank. He had been born in Pennsylvania on 14 Jan. 1843, and first served as a Private in the 1st Pennsylvania Artillery, and served continuously, even at one time as a hospital steward. He was discharged on 5 Oct. 1871 to attend medical school at Harvard, and graduated there in June 1875. By Ocober that year he was a contract surgeon for the U. S. Army. He was killed at the Little Big Horn at the age of 33. (Carroll and Price, pp. 165-66.)

badly, & we had lost a number. Lieut. McIntosh [91] &
De Rudio [92] were missing. McIntosh had been killed.
De Rudio escaped afterwards. Gerard, Reynolds, Herendine & Mich Boyer & Isaiah were missing from my
party. Gerard & Herendine escaped afterwards. The
others were dead. My Indian 1st Sergt., Bob-tailed
Bull,[93] and the Genl's. Bloody Knife, were also dead.

While we were straightening out matters we saw
a lot of fifteen dismounted men coming up the bluff
behind the timber. We moved to cover their approach
& found it was Herendine & soldiers who were left
dismounted in the timber and had made their way back
through the woods to the river & joined us. Two braves,
Half-Yellow-Face [94] and White Swan [95] were with us,

---

[91] Donald McIntosh was with Co. G, 7th Cav. He had been born in Canada
on 4 Sept. 1838, and was part blood Indian. He joined the 7th Cavalry in
1867. He was killed at the Little Big Horn a the age of 37. (Carroll and
Price, p. 142.)

[92] Charles Camilus De Rudio of Co. E, 7th Cav. (detailed TDY to Co. A)
was born in Italy on 26 Aug. 1832. Even though he had prior military service, having been educated in the Austrian Military Academy and serving
on the staff of Gen. Garibaldi in Italy, his career in the U. S. Army began
as a Private of Co. A, 79th New York Volunteers in Aug. 1864. He was
commissioned four months later as a 2nd Lieutenant in the U. S. Colored
Troops; but he was later mustered out on 5 Jan. 1866. He joined the 7th
Cav. on 14 July 1869, and rose to the rank of Captain. (Carroll and Price,
p. 125.) At the time Varnum identified him as missing, De Rudio was actually
hiding in the timber and brush in the valley, and later returned to Reno
Hill under cover of darkness.

[93] Bob Tailed Bull was killed in the valley fight at the Little Big Horn.
He was an Arikara scout who had first enlisted in the 7th Cav. at the age
of 45. He was one of the ten Indians engaged in the valley fight. (Hammer,
pp. 30-31.)

[94] Pvt. Half-Yellow-Face was a Crow Indian Scout who was in both the
valley and hilltop fights. He had enlisted in the 7th Inf. in April 1876, but
was on detached service with the 7th Cav. (Hammer, p. 34.)

[95] Pvt. White Swan, a Crow Indian scout, was wounded in the valley
fight at the Little Big Horn. He had enlisted in the 7th Inf. on 10 April
1876, but detached to the 7th Cav. He was severely wounded in the right
hand and leg (possibly by Whirlwind, a Cheyenne Indian) after crossing
the ford in the retreat. (Hammer, p. 40.)

the latter being wounded. Forked Horn [96] & Goose,[97] Ree scouts, the latter wounded, were also there. All the rest were gone.

Up the river we saw troops approaching, and a messenger was sent back on our line of approach to hurry up Troop B with the pack train. The troops from up the river proved to be Capt. F. W. Benteen [98] with Troop H, D & K, Capt. Weir, Lieuts. Godfrey, Gibson [99] & Edgerly.[100] B Troop with Capt. McDougall [101] & Lieut. Mathey [102] & the packs joined later.

[96] Pvt. Forked Horn was an Arikara scout. He was on his ninth enlistment at age of 37 on 27 April 1876. He was in the valley fight. He was the first to make contact with Col. Gibbon's men. (Hammer, p. 33.)

[97] Pvt. Goose was an Arikara scout who had been severely wounded in the retreat from the valley fight. Earlier he had participated in the Black Hills Expedition of 1874. (Hammer, p. 34.)

[98] Capt. Frederick William Benteen, commanding Co. H, 7th Cav., was born in Virginia in 1834. He had an illustrious career during the Civil War as an officer with the 10th Missouri Cav. He joined the 7th Cav. on 28 July 1866, and was in the Washita fight, and on the Yellowstone, Black Hills and Sioux campaigns. He was breveted a Brigadier General on 27 Feb. 1890 for action at the Little Big Horn. Later in the Nez Perce campaign. Died 22 June 1898 at the age of 63. (Carroll and Price, p. 117.) The lack of fondness Benteen held for Custer is legendary and has been the basis for much gossip, speculation and innuendos.

[99] Francis Marion Gibson was 1st Lieutenant in Co. H of the 7th Cav. at the Little Big Horn. He was born in Pennsylvania on 14 Dec. 1847. He retired from the service on 3 Dec. 1891. (Carroll and Price, p. 130.)

[100] Winfield Scott Edgerly was 2nd Lieutenant of Co. D, 7th Cav. at the Little Big Horn. He was born in New Hampshire on 29 May 1846, and graduated from the U. S. Military Academy in 1870. His was an illustrious career in the 7th Cav., serving it in many capacities. He survived the Little Big Horn fight. He later even served in Cuba. He retired as a Brigadier General on 29 Dec. 1909, but returned to active duty for a short while during World War I. (Carroll and Price, pp. 51-53.)

[101] Thomas Mower McDougall (son of Bvt. Brig. Gen. Charles McDougall, Surg., U. S. Army) was commanding Co. B, 7th Cav. at the Little Big Horn. He was born in Wisconsin on 21 May 1845. He received a commission as a 2nd Lieutenant when only 17 years old, and served honorably during the Civil War. After various assignments he did not join the 7th Cavalry until 1 Jan. 1871. He survived the Little Big Horn, and died on 3 July 1909, in Bradon, Vt., at the age of 64. (Carroll and Price, pp. 141-42.)

I, Varnum

The trail followed by Custer was found back from the bluffs & he must have been engaged in the valley from where I saw the gray horse troop.

When the command got together we followed the Custer trail to the highest point on the bluffs. Many scattered Indians were riding about at some distances, but the country was badly broken into gullies, and there was no sound of firing in any direction. We saw a lot of white objects scattered about which I thought were rocks but which we found afterwards were the naked bodies of Custer's men.

By this time, from every hill & vale, Indians were coming up the river towards us. Reno started to fall back along the bluffs to find a favorable place to stand them off, which was near where we came up from the valley. Reno & Benteen formed the line. Godfrey, with K Troop, dismounted, covering the movement. It was late in the P.M. when we were in shape and probably five thousand Indians attacked us. We had about three hundred men.

Our line formed a semi-circle from the crest of the bluff. It was very steep & high up from the river. Except across the middle point of the semi-circle we had a slight slope to cover us and across the low point made a sort of breast work of pack saddles. There were only one or two spades with the packs. We had the entire reserve supply of ammunition and plenty to eat and

---

102 Edward Gustave Mathey was 1st Lieutenant of Co. M (commanding pack train) at the Little Big Horn. He was born in France on 27 Oct. 1837. He enlisted as a Private in the 17th Indiana Volunteers in April 1861, and served later as 1st Sergeant. He was commissioned on 21 May 1862, and was engaged in many battles of the Civil War. He joined the 7th Cav. on 24 Sept. 1867. He survived the Little Big Horn, retired as a Lieutenant Colonel on 23 April 1904. (Carroll and Price, pp. 142-43.)

some grain for stock, but water was almost inaccessible.

Near the center we placed the animals in a circle tied to each other and in the center of that placed our wounded. We had our Dr. Porter.[103] The Indians fired at us from behind a circle of hills varying from 2 to 5 hundred yards range. They would pour lead into us for fifteen to thirty minutes, and then charge us mounted. We lay low while they were firing & when they charged we sat up and let them have it and drove them back. This they kept up incessantly as long as they could see until the night of the 26th.

We had little to fear from them during the night as they have a superstition I believe against being killed in the darkness. It was fortunate for us for they could have ridden us down at night with small loss to them.

We managed to get a few canteens of water that night and the following day from the river, but it was very risky work. We had a few cans of tomatoes among our stores also. These and the water was mostly consumed by the wounded.

As I had no sleep for forty-eight hours, I went to sleep about midnight. I was awakened by being carried & found myself in the arms of Pvt. "Tony" Sie-

---

103 Henry Renaldo Porter was Act. Asst. Surg., attached to Headquarters, at the time of the Little Big Horn. He had been born at New York Mills, N.Y., on 3 Feb. 1848. He graduated from the Georgetown Univ. School of Medicine in 1872, and at once presented his skills and services to the U. S. Army. He had served with the 5th Cav. in the Apache Campaign before joining, as contract surgeon, the personnel at Camp Hancock on 1 Dec. 1874. He then contracted on 14 May 1876 for the Sioux Campaign and was the surgeon of record during the hilltop fight at the Little Big Horn on Reno Hill. (Carroll and Price, pp. 167-68.) Dr. Porter's final resting place is the only one amongst the officers of the 7th Cavalry on duty at the Little Big Horn which has never been discovered. It is believed his body was cremated, but no official office in the United States or in India has been able to get this confirmed.

belder,[104] Troop A, who, when firing opened in the morning about 3 o'clock, found me in a very exposed position. He laid me down & I slept for a while & felt better. I was up by sunrise. During the forenoon we were bothered by two or three Indians who got a position on the edge of the bluff, down the stream, and at about 100 yards range & when they fired they got some one. At Benteen's suggestion, the troops on that flank charged them. We were opened on by the whole circle. I felt a pain in both legs at once, and thought for a second I had lost both legs. I got a bullet through the calf of one leg, and as my foot was up, while I was running, the other went down my leg cutting the yellow stripes off my trousers and denting the leather of my boot over the ankle bone. It did not touch my person, but acted like a blow on my ankel bone and the foot swelled up, turned black & blue and was really the worst wound of the two.

We had no trouble after that from that quarter. I dropped into a shallow trench when I got back and tried to examine the hole in my leg to see how bad it was, but every time I did so, a bullet cut the dirt very near it.

A young private of B Troop got to laughing at my endeavors, and while doing so a bullet went from the top of his head down through his body. He probably never knew what happened to him.[105] I afterwards met

---

104 This was Pvt. Anton Siebelder who had been born in Lichewald, Germany. He was on his second enlistment at the time of the Little Big Horn. He was discharged on 2 April 1877, but re-enlisted on 17 Dec. 1877, following the Nez Perce Campaign. He was finally discharged on 20 Dec. 1882. (Hammer, p. 55.)

105 There is no way of knowing exactly who this soldier was, but Co. B lost only two privates killed, Pvts. Richard B. Dorn and George B. Mask. Hammer states only that Dorn was killed, not citing where, and Mask being

the man on the other side of me. He was a youngster in St. Paul, Minn., driving me to the R. R. depot. He noticed my name on my trunk and made himself known by telling this story.

In the P.M. I made a proposition to Maj. Reno that if he would let me go and take one companion, I would try and get through the lines that night and carry word of our fix to any troops I could reach. He refused. He said I used a gun too well to be spared. He finally agreed to let the scouts go if they would. They promised, but I don't think they ever started or tried. They brought back the dispatches and said there were too many Indians. At the time they started the Indians had probably left.

That evening all was quiet and everybody seemed to be of the opinion that troops were coming to our assistance and that the Indians had gone. We sounded trumpets giving the various calls to warn any troops when close. We changed our position so that the up-stream end of our position became the down-stream end, fortified as best we could.

We got nearer the water and after midnight sent horses down to water, a few at a time. About midnight, Fred Gerard and one of the Jackson boys came into our lines. They had been left in the woods and escaped up the river in the dark. Before morning De Rudio and Private O'Neil [106] also came in. They had been left

killed on the hilltop fight, so it is very probable it was the latter about whom Varnum spoke.

106 This was Pvt. Thomas O'Neill from Dublin, Ireland, and of Co. G, 7th Cav. He had been missing after the valley fight, but rejoined on Reno Hill. He was a cook for Lt. McIntosh in the Sioux Campaign until the battle. He was discharged in June 1877, thereby missing the Nez Perce Campaign, but re-enlisted after the troops left on that campaign. He was finally discharged at Fort Snelling on 14 July 1882. (Hammer, p. 147.)

when the others had escaped up the river with Gerard & Jackson, but became separated.

On the morning of the 27th there were no Indians in sight. The horses were all watered and fed, and we did what we could for the wounded. That something was happening we knew. We had no means to move our wounded, even if not interrupted by hostiles.

About 9 o'clock a body of men were seen coming up the valley. Whether troops or Indians could not be made out, but soon it developed into troops. Six companies of the 7th Infantry and four troops 2d Cavalry with Genl. Terry in command was marching to our relief. The Genl. & staff came up to us & the troops camped in the valley. They told us that Custer and the five troops with him were all dead, and their naked bodies mutilated & scalped were down the river about three or four miles. Such a scene! I will not try to describe it. Our brother officers and dearest friends butchered and scalped!

We commenced at once to remove the wounded to the 7th Infty. camp. Surgeons got to work. Saddler Madden [107] had to have his leg amputated at the thigh. The ground with a piece of shelter tent to lie on was the operating table. He was a pretty hard drinker, but not had a drop of liquor for months. Ether had no

---

[107] Saddler Michael P. Madden of Co. K, 7th Cav., was wounded in the leg, the only one to have suffered any injury, during that heroic effort of men who placed their lives on the line and worked their way to the river to bring back water for the wounded and dying. Madden's wound was in the right leg (double fracture below the knee). Dr. Porter amputated his leg on the battlefield. He was born in Galcony, Ireland, and was on his second enlistment at the time of the Little Big Horn. He was discharged on 28 Aug. 1876 at Fort Lincoln, and later was employed in the harness depot at the Department of Dakota in St. Paul. (Hammer, pp. 190-91.) His death and burial site are unknown. However, of all, he should have been awarded the Medal of Honor as were so many of his friends for their bravery in the water parties. He was never nominated for that honor, probably because he had left the service before they were nominated and confirmed.

effect on him. "Give me a drink and cut away," he said. They did, & when ready to commence they gave another. He stood it all right and when asked how he felt he said, "Give me a drink & you can cut off the other."

Everything but the troops was moved that day, and on the morning of the 28th, we started to bury the dead. Only a few spades could be procured and the bodies were covered with earth just as they lay. The officers were all identified except Lieuts. Harrington[108] & Sturgis.[109] The officers' bodies were buried in shallow graves & marked. We then marched to the camp of the other troop. In the meanwhile the Infantry had buried the bodies who fell in Reno's first attack. These bodies were horribly mangled. Indian travois had been made to haul the wounded, but some had to be carried in extemporized hand litters. Capt. Keogh's[110] horse,

---

[108] Henry Moore Harrington was 2nd Lieutenant of Co. C. of the 7th Cav. at the Little Big Horn. He had been born in New York on 30 April 1849, attended the U. S. Military Academy, and was graduated from there on 14 June 1872. He was on the Yellowstone and Black Hills expeditions and was killed at the Little Big Horn. (Carroll and Price, pp. 64-65.)

[109] James Garland Sturgis, son of Col. Samuel D. Sturgis, also of the 7th Cav., was 2nd Lieutenant of Co. M, on TDY to Co. E, at the time of the battle. He was born in New Mexico on 24 Jan. 1854, attended the U. S. Military Academy, and graduated there on 16 June 1875, and was assigned to his father's command. This was his first major expedition, and he was killed at the Little Big Horn at the age of 22. (Carroll and Price, p. 101.) His body was never found. Camp James G. Surgis, on the northwest slope of Bear Butte, D.T., was established on 1 July 1878, and named in his honor. (Hammer, p. 222.)

[110] Myles Walter Keogh was the Captain commanding Co. I, 7th Cav. at the Little Big Horn. He had been born in Ireland on 25 March 1842. In the 1860's he was a 2nd Lieutenant in the Battalion of St. Patrick of the Papal Army. Three month's later he was commissioned a Lieutenant in the Papal Guards. During the Civil War his first assignment was Captain, Additional Aide-de-Camp to Gen. Shields. He later served on the staff of Gen. Buford. His highest rank attained was Brevet Lieutenant Colonel. He joined the 7th Cav. on 28 July 1866, and was killed at the Little Big Horn at the age of 34. (Carroll and Price, p. 138.)

I, Varnum

Comanche,[111] was found alive on Custer field, but badly wounded. We managed to get him along with us and he was cured & kept till he died at Fort Riley, Kans.,[112] in 1891, I believe.

We moved down the stream a few miles that day, and on the 29th, in the night, when it was cool, on account of the wounded we marched about 20 miles to the Big Horn at the mouth of the Little Big Horn, where a steamboat, the *Far West*,[113] waited. Capt. Grant Marsh [114] had pushed its way. It was very welcome.

I had lost all my baggage, and I managed to get a suit of underwear from the officers of Co. B, 6th Infantry, and shave and clean up a bit. Having embarked the wounded, we marched down the Big Horn to the Yellowstone and were ferried to the north bank where we encamped. An Irishman of Troop A went crazy here and had to be tied & sent to an insane asylum.

One troop of Cavalry, with Genl. Terry & staff, went down the river by boat to the camp at Powder river.

---

111 Comanche, the horse that was found on the Custer battlefield, and has been the inspiration for dozens of poems, books and art, has generated much romanticism about the battle. For fuller studies see Anthony A. Amaral, *Comanche,* Los Angeles, 1961; Barron Brown, *Comanche,* Kansas City, 1935; David Dary, *Comanche,* Lawrence, Ks., 1976; and possibly the most famous, Edward S. Luce, *Keogh, Comanche and Custer,* pvtly. printed, 1939. There are, of course, many other worthy references.

112 Camp Center Ks., was established on 17 May 1853, on the north bank of the Kansas River at the junction of the Smoky Hill and Republican forks near present-day Junction City, Kansas. The name was changed to Fort Riley on 27 June 1853. (Prucha, p. 102. *See also* Billings, Circular No. 4, pp. 287-290 and Circular No. 8, pp. 285-87, and W. F. Pride, *The History of Fort Riley,* pvtly. printed, 1926.)

113 *Far West* was the steamboat which figured so prominently in the history of the 7th Cav. and the history of steamboating on the Missouri. She was used variously as a troop transport, supply transport and sadly, the return of the wounded of the 7th Cav. to Fort Abraham Lincoln.

114 Grant Marsh was the Captain of the *Far West.* For detailed information on this important figure see Joseph Mills Hanson, *The Conquest of the Missouri,* Chicago, 1909.

I was taken along. I had mustered my detachment on the 30th of June & dropped twenty scouts as "missing in action." I found them all at Powder River, and they were paid on the rolls on which they were dropped.

I was placed in charge of our wagon train, and with the Infantry at the camp as guard we were ferried to the north bank of the Yellowstone and marched up the river and met the other troops at the mouth of the Rosebud.

The 7th Cavalry was reorganized soon. Major Reno appointed commander, Lieut. Geo. D. Wallace, now a 1st Lieut., as Adjutant, and Lieut. W. S. Edgerly, now a 1st Lieut., as quartermaster, in place of Lieut. Cooke, killed in action, and Nowlan, promoted. I became a 1st Lieut. vice Calhoun,[115] killed in action, which took me to Troop C. But a troop was formed temporarily from the remnants of three of the troops which were with Custer. Some of the men had been with the pack train & some with the wagon train, and a batch of recruits had been left at Powder river without horses. Horses for these had arrived, and thirty of this detachment made a fair troop. I was placed in command in addition to my other duties.

Col. Nelson A. Miles [116] arrived with six companies

---

115 James Calhoun (Custer's brother-in-law) was 1st Lieutenant of Co. C, 7th Cav., on TDY commanding Co. L at the Little Big Horn. He was born in Ohio on 24 Aug. 1845. His military career began as a Private in Co. D of the 23rd Inf. (1865-1867), and then commissioned 2nd Lieutenant in the 32nd Inf. on 31 July 1867. He was assigned to the 7th Cav. on 1 Jan. 1871. He was killed at the Little Big Horn at the age of 30. (Carroll and Price, p. 121.)

116 Nelson Appleton Miles was born in Massachusetts, and entered the service as a 1st Lieutenant in the 22nd Massachusetts Inf. on 9 Sept. 1861, and rose rapidly through the ranks, culminating as Commander of the U. S. Army. He retired from the army on 8 Aug. 1903, and died in 1925. (Heitman, pp. 708-09.) Suggested readings: Nelson A. Miles, *Serving the Republic*, N.Y., 1911, and *Personal Recollections of . . .* , N.Y., 1896.

of the 5th Infantry and Lieut. Col. E. S. Otis,[117] with six companies of the 22d Infantry. The entire command was ferried to the south bank and were once more at our starting point in the valley of the Rosebud. We had our wagon train and two pieces of artillery. We marched for two or three days up the Rosebud when, while on the march, we observed a cloud of dust come in view, coming towards us. The train was halted and closed up. The 5th Infty. on our flank, and the 22d on the other, formed a skirmish line on the crest of the bluffs. Other Infty. troops covered the front & rear of the train. The 7th Cavalry (what was left of it) formed a mounted skirmish line across the valley. Four troops of the 2d Cavalry were held in line in rear of our skirmish line and the two guns unlimbered for action. The Crow scouts, stripped almost naked, went racing to the front. Genl. Terry and staff were an a conspicuous knoll.

In forming line, the 7th Cav. was pretty well advanced up the valley. I with provisional troop, was about center. Soon some of the Crows came racing back, and as they passed through my line were shouting "maenschita, maenschita," (the spelling is my own). I recognized the word but for the life of me I could not think what it meant. The cloud of dust continued to approach when out of its volume a small cloud came rapidly to the front and Buffalo Bill [118] came in view.

---

[117] Elwell Stephen Otis was born in Maryland and first joined the service as a Captain in the 140th New York Inf. on 13 Sept. 1862. His highest rank, brevet, was Major General. He retired from the service on 25 March 1902. Before his retirement he served in the Dept. of the Pacific as Commander, and then the Military Governor of the Philippines (1898-1900), and was instrumental in the suppression of the Philippine Insurrection. (Heitman, p. 762.)

He reined his horse back on his haunches, and taking off his sombrero, gave us a grand salute. We had certainly given him a grand parade to receive him.

My troop was ordered to report to Genl. Terry as escort and rode away guided by Buffalo Bill to call on Genl. Crook, who was approaching with ten troops 5th Cavy., ten of the 3d, four of the 2d, and a body of Infantry composed of detachments from the 4th & 14th & probably some others. I have forgotten his strength.

After the interview, the two commands went into camp. Next day our wagon train was sent back to the river with an Infantry guard and we all took to our pack mules again. Crook's command was with packs only. We now had an army big enough to whip all the Indians in the United States, but we saw no more Indians till we arrived at an agency.

We marched to the mouth of the Powder river. In a day or two Crook started east and we followed up the Powder, but before night Buffalo Bill came into camp again with some sick & disabled officers & men. He had started down the Yellowstone by steamboat to rejoin his show in the East. On the way down they discovered that a lot of Indians were crossing to the north bank, and he got a horse which was fortunately on the boat and rode back during the night to notify us.

Word was sent to Genl. Crook, and we marched to the Yellowstone again, & were ferried to the north bank. General Miles, with the 5th Infty., was detached to build a cantonment at mouth of Tongue river, after-

---

[118] William Frederick Cody, aka Buffalo Bill, and first called that by E. Z. C. Judson (Ned Buntline), was born in 1846 and died in 1917. Two extremely valuable biographies are suggested: Don Russell, *The Lives And Legends Of Buffalo Bill*, Norman, 1960; and Nellie Snyder Yost, *Buffalo Bill: His Family, Friends, Fame, Failures and Fortunes*, Chicago, 1979.

wards named Fort Keogh.[119] We marched across to the Missouri river at Poplar creek, were ferried to the north bank, and then marched to Fort Buford. Our wagon train had joined us, but a great portion was left at Buford for Miles' command. The 22d was left on the Yellowstone guarding supply trains. The 7th Cavalry marched to Fort A. Lincoln, arriving in September after a campaign of 2500 miles or more.

Here we got recruits to fill our troops up to 100 men each. New horses arrived also, and saddles & other equipment. 1st Lieut. Henry Jackson [120] had become Captain of Troop C, of which I had become 1st Lieut. I was still on duty as Chief of Scouts & had these to reorganize, but Capt. Jackson had been on duty in the Signal Corps in Washington for years and needed my help very badly. We were to get in shape for another campaign right away.

I worked from reveille until after dark every day and wrote up papers to settle dead mens' accounts at night. 2d Lieut. H. G. Sickel [121] soon joined from West

---

[119] Fort Keogh, Mt., was a site occupied on 28 Aug. 1876, at the mouth of the Tongue River at present-day Miles City, Mt., which was officially established as a military post on 11 Sept. 1876. It was part of the movement of troops into the area after the Custer massacre. The post was known as Cantonment on Tongue River, as New Post on the Yellowstone, and as Tongue River Barracks. On 8 Nov. 1877 it was named Fort Keogh. (Prucha, p. 82.)

[120] Henry Jackson, born in England on 31 May 1837, was absent on detached service in Wash., D. C., since 9 Aug. 1871, and therefore had not participated in any of the campaigns of the 7th Cav., though he had transferred from the 5th U. S. Colored Troops to the 7th Cav. on 28 July 1866. By 1901, he had risen to the rank of Colonel and retired on 31 May 1901. (Carroll and Price, p. 136.)

[121] Horatio Gates Sickel, Jr., was born in Pennsylvania. He graduated from the U. S. Military Academy in 1876 and was immediately assigned to the 7th Cav. He saw duty on the frontier from that time to 1893. He was in the Spanish-American War and in the Philippine Insurrection. (Cullum, p. 272.)

Point, and I was soon afterwards put in command of Troop I, which had been Keogh's, and to which Capt. H. J. Nowlan had been promoted. He had been the quartermaster of the expedition and had not yet joined.

Genl. Sturgis joined about this time & took command of the regiment & post. Four troops under Major Reno were sent down the west bank of the Missouri river to dismount the agency Indians on the lower Missouri. Genl. Sturgis took the other eight troops & marched down the east bank. I was with this latter command. We went as far down as the Cheyenne Agency and gathered a thousand or more ponies and got no arms of any value.

The ponies were driven east and a great many escaped, or were lost or stolen & the balance sold for the benefit of the Indians. It was quite a blow to them. F Troop went east with the herd and wintered at Fort Abercrombie [122] near the Minnesota line. The balance of us marched back to Fort A. Lincoln, arriving about Nov. 1st. C Troop was slated to go to Fort Totten [123] on the Canadian boundary, and I did not anticipate the march with any degree of pleasure.

The Missouri river was impassable for running ice, and they were waiting for it to freeze over so we could

---

[122] Fort Abercrombie, N.D., was built on the west bank of the Red River of the North at the approximate head of navigation, about twelve miles north of the present city of Wahpeton, N.D., in the vicinity of a place known as Graham's Point, Mn. This post was set up on 28 Aug. 1858, then abandoned in 1859, but reoccupied in 1860. Troops were finally withdrawn on 23 Oct. 1877. (Prucha, p. 55. *See also* Billings, Circular No. 4, pp. 372-77, and Circular No. 8, pp. 389-92.)

[123] Fort Totten was established on 17 July 1867, on the southeast shore of Devil's Lake, as part of the plan to place the Indians of the region on a reservation and as one of the posts to protect the overland route from Minnesota to Montana. (Prucha, p. 112. *See also* Billings, Circular No. 4, pp. 383-86, and Circular No. 8, pp. 444-49.)

cross on the ice. I had closed up my scout papers and I Troop papers and was at Headquarters putting on some finishing touches when Genl. Sturgis came in and asked me how I would like to be Regimental Quartermaster. Wallace & Edgerly, appointed by Reno, had resigned when the Colonel joined. Wallace was retained as Adjutant and on Nov. 14th, 1876, I was made R. Q. M. and ordered to duty as Post Q. M. and at once assumed my new duties. So I did not have to go to Totten after all. Wallace and I immediately filled up a set of quarters. Lieut. Hare also lived with us. We started a mess and had so many young officers and guests that we generally had to set the table twice to accommodate them all. For quite a while Major Merrill [124] with his wife & two daughters messed with us till they could get settled.

The winter passed quietly; the weather was intensely cold. The contract for cottonwood was not let until winter, and green cottonwood would not burn, so the troops had to gather any driftwood on the banks of the river and in the river bottoms to keep us from freezing. The thermometer in January dropped as low as -50°. A lot of half-starved mules was brought in from up the river for recuperation and I had very poor shelter for them and had to build frame shelters & cover them with stable manure. I was also busy preparing army wagons and toward spring received a lot of new mules and fifty new army wagons, and was ordered to fit up a train of forty-six mule teams and load with grain &

---

[124] Lewis Merrill of Pennsylvania graduated from the U. S. Military Academy in 1855, and immediately assigned as 2nd Lieutenant to the 2nd Dragoons. Highest rank attained was brevet Brigadier General. He saw much service on the frontier, especially in the Nez Perce Campaign. (Heitman, p. 705, and Cullum, p. 249.)

send to Fort Buford. The train got away in April with Lieut. A. L. Wagner,[125] 6th Infty., in charge.

The frost was just coming out of the ground & the roads so bad that the mules consumed about all the oats.

[End of existing written narrative]

Editor's note – Lt. Varnum evidently began to write – or perhaps rewrite – this narrative. That which follows is apparently one of the later drafts, addressing itself only to the battle, and even though it contains approximately the same information which appears in the previous version, there are sufficient differences to warrant the repetition. In any event, it is short and also incomplete. To the regret of all, Lieutenant Varnum – or most likely a Colonel at the time of the writing of both drafts – never completed any of his narratives. In the second draft printed here, his handwriting becomes almost unreadable at times, and this is especially true when describing the battle. It seems as if his heart and mind raced just a little faster than did his pen.

Second Draft of the Custer Battle Narrative

Returning to Fort Abraham Lincoln, Dak. Terty. in April, 1876, from "leave of absence," I was detailed to organize, enlist and command a detachment of Indian scouts for the Expedition of Genl. A. H. Terry against hostile Sioux Indians. I enlisted about sixty-five. Two or three were old Sioux scouts, and the balance, Ree Indians including four half-breed Ree-whites. Fred Gerard was Ree interpreter. A negro, Isaiah, was Sioux interpreter. Charley Reynolds & the Ree, Bloody Knife, were employed as guides and attached to my command.

---

[125] Arthur Lockwood Wagner of Illinois graduated from the U. S. Military Academy in 1875, and was immediately assigned to frontier duty to 1881. Later he was on the staff of General Miles. He participated in the Philippine Insurrection. He died, a Colonel, in North Carolina, on 17 June 1905, at the age of 52. (Cullum, p. 271.)

I, Varnum

The command left Fort A. Lincoln about the middle of May, and consisted of the scouts, the 7th Cavalry, and about a regiment of Infantry composed of parts of the 6th & 17th Regts., two pieces of artillery and a large wagon train.

The line of march was along the N.P.R.R. survey till we crossed the Little Missouri River when we turned in a southerly direction & struck the Powder River about twenty-five or thirty miles above the mouth. The march was uneventful. I was generally attached to & marched with the 7th Cavalry. I was 2d Lieutenant of Troop A, and messed with my Capt., M. Moylan.

From the Powder River Major Reno, with a squadron of the 7th Cavalry & some Indian scouts, was sent south on a scout in search of the hostiles. I do not know what his instructions were. He left his wagons and took pack mules only. The remainder of the command marched down the right bank of the Powder to the Yellowstone. Here the train was parked and left with an Infantry guard and the rest of the command took pack animals only and marched up the right bank of the Yellowstone to the mouth of Tongue river, and here, on the site of Miles City of today, Reno rejoined us.

We then marched to the mouth of the Rosebud. Genl. Terry was there on a steamboat. Genl. Gibbon, with six companies of the 7th Infantry, and a squadron of four troops of the 2d Cavalry, arrived from the Montana Military posts, having marched down the Yellowstone.

Long conferences took place between Genls. Terry, Gibbon & Custer on the steamboat, and on the 22d of June Genl. Custer with the 7th Cavalry and Indian scouts and pack trains started up the Rosebud. I had furnished a number of detachments of scouts to carry mail & dispatches, and when I left on the 22d I had twenty-five Ree Indians including three half-breeds. My two interpreters, Charlie Reynolds & Bloody Knife & in addition six Crow Indian scouts from Genl. Gibbon's command and Mich Boyer, Crow interpreter, & a guide named Herendine.

We did not get away till near noon, as I remember, and made only a short march on the 22d. My detachment did the advance guard work and covered the entire valley. The Crow Indians acted under the direct supervision of General Custer & I saw little of them till the night of the 24th. On the 23rd we made a long march. We struck not only the trail of the Indians but the entire valley of the Rosebud appeared to have been a camp, where they had moved along as the grass was grazed off. There had evidently been buffalo in the country and frames for drying meat and the remains of camp fires where meat bones infected by maggots, & half-dried pony dung indicated recent presence of the Indian.

I was always way ahead of the command with my scouts and was especially instructed to look out for any trails leaving the main trail up the river & going eastward. After we had marched about twenty miles on the 24th, an orderly reported to me that the General wanted to see me. The command had halted. I went back and reported. The General told me that Lieut. Godfrey had reported that a large travois trail had left the main trail about ten miles back, and gone eastward up a branch creek heading into the Rosebud from that direction. I told him that I had covered the front with scouts and was up & down my line all the time & had half-breeds who could talk English along, and that I did not believe it possible. After considerable discussion I was ordered to go back to the branch stream referred to & investigate. I went & found that the branch stream had strip cut banks and the main travois trail had gone up the branch to find a suitable crossing & had then crossed the branch & returned to the valley of the Rosebud. I had therefore had my extra 20 miles ride for nothing.

The General said I needed an assistant and detailed Lieut. L. R. Hare to report to me & help me out. We marched thirty or more miles that day, & how many I put in on that day's work, riding my front and going back, I can only guess, but certainly more than fifty.

After we camped, the Crow Indians came in and had a long talk with the General in a clump of trees near my camp. The General then sent for me. He told me that the Crows had reported to him that there was a high hill in the divide between the Rosebud & Little Big Horn and that this was a "Crow Nest" near the top, and that when the Sioux were in the country the Crows used this to watch the Sioux, when they (the Crows) were on pony-stealing expeditions against the Sioux. That their mounts could be hid in the Crow Nest and from the top of the hill, when daylight broke in the morning, the air was still and clear, and they could tell whether the Indians were in camp on the Little Big Horn.

The Crows were to leave about 9 o'clock and go to the hill and he (the General) wanted an intelligent white man to go with them & get their report & put it on paper & send it back to him. "Well, I guess that means me," I replied. He said I had had a hard day & he did not want to order me on such a duty anyway.

I said, "Well, you detailed me to command the scouts. It is my place to go & I would not feel complimented if you sent any one else," or words to that effect. He said he would like to have me go, & in fact wanted me to if I felt able. I told him I wanted some one white man to talk to and asked for Charlie Reynolds. I took the five Crows, about a dozen Rees & Boyer, the Crow interpreter. He said he would break camp about eleven o'clock and move up to the base of the hills and bivouac in the ravines till he heard from me. I took the Rees as messengers.

We left at 9 o'clock P.M. and arrived at the Crow Nest about two o'clock A.M. on the 25th. It was a long mean ride in the darkness. I lay down & got about an hour's sleep & then climbed to the crest of the hill where I found the Crows. I could see down the valley of a stream flowing into the Little Big Horn, two teepees, one partly wrecked or fallen over. The Crows said there was a big village in the valley of the Little Big Horn behind a line of bluffs & pointed to a large pony herd. I could not see it. They said, "Look for worms on the grass." But I could see nothing.

The Indians called my attention to smoke rising from where Custer had bivouacked & did not like it. About five o'clock I wrote a note to the General & sent it off by the Rees, telling him the information I got from the Crows. Soon after this I saw an Indian, mounted, leading a pony on a long lariat, & a boy, also mounted, riding behind. They were riding parallel to the divide and evidently heading for a gap to cross the ridge. The Crows wanted them headed off & killed. Reynolds, Boyer, two Crows & myself started off to do it. We got into a tangle of ravines. We heard a sound of Crow calls from the hill. Our Crows answered & then we turned back. I asked Boyer what it meant and he did not know.

On returning we found the Indian had changed his course, but soon afterwards he did cross the divide & went down the slope towards Custer's advancing column. We could see the dust of the column, but not the troops at that time. This Indian continued on a long distance & then stopped for a while & suddenly disappeared. He had evidently discovered the advance of the troops.

Later I saw seven Indians in single file riding on the crest of a ridge running north from the divide & parallel to Custer's advance. Outlined against the sky three ponies looked as large as elephants. Suddenly they disappeared, but two black spots reappeared. Evidently they also had seen the troops & the two black spots were Indians watching them.

About ten o'clock the column was in sight heading for a low spot in the divide where the trail crosses. I rode out to meet the troops, but met General Custer & Tom (his brother). He sent Tom back and rode to the Crow Nest with me. I reported to him all I had seen and what the Crows claimed to have seen. We climbed to the crest of the hill and the Genl. talked with the Crows thru Boyer. The General finally said, "I have got mighty good eyes and I can see no Indians," & Boyer replied, "If you can't find more Indians in that valley than you ever saw together before, you may hang me." The General replied, "It would do a damn sight of good to hang you, wouldn't it?" This was the second time I ever heard Custer use such an expression, the other being in an Indian fight in 1873.

We rode back to the command and I hunted for food & drink. The officers were called together and the situation discussed, but I was not present. The command then resumed the march. I went ahead to the left front, Lieut. Hare covering the right front. I got into the hills & a long way from the command, & when at last I rejoined, Major Reno with three troops of the 7th Cavy. was passing in front at the trot. I reported to the General saying I guess he could see about all I could of the situation. "I don't know. What can you see?" said the General. "The whole valley in front is full of Indians," I replied, "& you can see them when you take that rise," (pointing to the right front).

I asked where Reno was going & he told me he was to attack. I asked if I was to go with him. He said I might. Fred Gerard, the interpreter, shouted a lot of Indian language to the scouts & we started at the gallop. My classmate, Lt. Wallace, was riding with the General as topographical officer. I turned back & shouted to him, "Come on, Nick, don't stay back with the coffee coolers." Custer laughed & made a sign to Wallace who joined me. Lieut. Hare also joined, and with the scouts & attackers we rode to overtake Reno which we did as he was fording the stream & came out into the open valley ahead & covered the advance with my scouts, Lts. Wallace & Hare, Charlie Reynolds, Herendine, Boyer & Fred Gerard & Bloody Knife, with myself, leading but spread out across the front.

The Indians were spread across the valley, riding madly in every direction, sometimes apparently about to charge and then turning & running away only to return again. As we were nearing their village I looked back & saw the command dismounting to fight on foot, and we all rode back behind the lines. I joined my

I, Varnum

Troop A. As I joined I happened to look towards the high bluffs on the other side of the river & saw the gray horse Troop E, in column, going down stream. The conformation of the ground on the bluff was such that I could see only that much of the column.

The right of our line rested on a timbered bottom. A cut bank about four feet high surrounded the timber on the side away from the river. I heard some one say the Indians were getting around to our rear & would get our led horses. They had been placed in the timber. I rode down into the woods & worked my way to the horses & brought them close up to the line, but still in the timber. As I was returning I saw G Troop going back through the woods & met Lieut. Hodgson who was Reno's adjutant. He was following G Troop. He said Reno was going to attack the village with G Troop. He was worried about his horse that I thought had been wounded. I saw no sign of it however. I rode to the troops, but had to dismount & tie my horse to a tree as the brush was so thick.

The skirmish had apparently swung back on the timber & heavy firing & constant. Men were going back to the horses for more ammunition. I met Reynolds & Gerard & asked how things were going. Reynolds said pretty bad, or words to that effect. Gerard pulled out a half-pint flask & said, "Well, we may never have a chance. Let's take a drink." Before I could do so, men were falling back into the timber & calling out, "They are going to charge."

I ran to my horse. The rush of mounted men forced me into a by-path and I got out at the rear of the column. The command was on the run. A front of ten or a dozen men way ahead of me, and men twos, threes

& by file tell they were rods apart at the rear, all riding along the timber and towards the bluff on the other bank. I was on a thoroughbred horse from the Kentucky race tracks & soon overtook the column. Indians rode along the column with their Winchester rifles across the pommel of their saddles, pumping them as fast as possible. I got to the head of the column just as it reached the stream. There was no ford, but we jumped in & climbed out the best we could.

Reno and Moylan were the only officers I recall seeing at that time. I started up a steep ridge heading to my left. The main column took me to the right. The men to the right called to me to come back. I did not see why, but came back.

The horse of a wounded soldier was killed & Sergt. Culbertson [126] & I caught a loose M Troop horse & put the wounded man on it & we went up with the troops. Dr. De Wolf started up where I did, followed by his orderly. Those above me called to him to come back. He turned to see what was the matter & a bullet from the top of the bluff killed him. His orderly joined the column.

1st Sergt. Heyn,[127] Troop A, had a bullet through his knee & Sergt. Culbertson & I helped him to the top of the bluffs. Not long after our arrival we saw a number of dismounted men, about fifteen, I believe, coming out of the woods to the bluffs and along the bluffs near

---

[126] Sgt. Culbertson, Co. A, was in both the valley and hilltop fights. He was born in Pittsburgh, and at the time of the fight was in his second enlistment. Later that year, in September, he was reduced to rank of Private by Captain Moylan for failing to extinguish a camp fire. He testified at the Reno Court of Inquiry in 1879. (Hammer, p. 47.)

[127] William Heyn was 1st Sergeant of Co. A, and was in both the valley and hilltop fights. He had been born in Bremen, Germany. He is sometimes listed on rolls as Hynes. (Hammer, p. 47.)

the river. We moved down stream, or some of us did, to cover them from any Indian attack, and they joined us led by the scout, Herendine. The Indians had left us for the time being.

Messengers were sent to the pack train to hurry it up. Col. Benteen with three troops was seen coming down the river from above where we had crossed, and he joined with Troops D (Weir), H (Benteen) & K (Godfrey). Captain McDougal [sic], with Troop B & the pack train also joined us. Col. Reno learned that Lieut. Hodgson had been killed where we crossed the river & went down to the crossing with some men. I learned of it only when he was returning.

We had a number of badly wounded men & to move, they had to be carried in blankets. We had no stretchers. The command moved down the river along the top of the bluffs, following Custer's trail, which we found.

After helping with the wounded I joined Capt. Weir with the advance. We moved to a point that overlooked where Custer's fight took place, but it was covered with Indians riding in every direction. A considerable firing was heard but there was no body of troops in sight. I saw some white objects that I thought were rocks, but found afterwards they were naked bodies of men. We fell back along the bluff and the Indians swarmed back on us. A dimounted skirmish line was formed by Lt. Godfrey with K Troop covering the movement. A place was selected for the final stand and everything brought inside the lines.

These formed irregular semi-circle back from the edge of the bluff. The horses & mules were tied to each other. The wounded men were placed among the horses for cover. Here we fought it out.

I was thoroughly exhausted. I had ridden about seventy miles on the 24th and had only about an hour's sleep at the Crow Nest that night. About 10 o'clock I lay down on the edge of the bluffs and must have gone to sleep at once. I was awakened by being carried somewhere, and found myself in the arms of old "Tony" Siebelder of Troop A. It seems I had gone to sleep at an exposed point and when daylight broke, old "Tony" saw my danger & was carrying me to a safer place to finish my sleep.

But I had had enough and got busy with my gun on the firing line. I joined the men on the line looking down the river. The Indians behind ridges at from about two to five or six hundred yards poured lead into us for twenty or thirty minutes, and then charged us, mounted. We did not return this fire except to get their range. The men were ready, however, with their sights set, and when the charge came, our reply came also and was so effective that it stopped the charge. This was repeated again & again, all day long.

A few Indians got cover, near the bluff, about two hundred yards down stream, and their fire was very effective. Benteen came over from the up-stream front & suggested we charge them. With a yell we went to it, & that ended all fire from that point.

I caught a bullet through the flesh of my leg, and another struck my ankle bone on the other foot. This last one only dented the leather of my boot but became the worst of the two wounds. It acted like a blow of a hammer on my ankle bone, & made me very lame for several days.

Returning from the charge I dropped into a shallow trench with a private of M Troop. Feeling blood running down my leg I tried to pull my boot off with the other foot while lying on my back. A bullet struck the dirt near my hill, & I dropped my foot. My companion chuckled. I turned on my side and tried again with the same result. I called him a damned chucklehead & just then a charge of Indians set us at work with our carbines.

My wound was not examined till the following day. I later in the day went to Capt. Moylan's line & with other officers talked over our situation. I suggested I would try and get away during the night if I could get a good man to go with me & carry the news & try to get relief. I talked to Herendine, but he thought it too risky. Sergt. Geo. McDermott [128] of A Troop (killed at Bear Paw in 1877) agreed to go with me & I went to see Major Reno about it. He was with Capt. Weir. I made my proposition to him. He did not reply for some time & then said he could not afford to lose two good shots & that we would get killed anyway. I said we might as well get killed trying to get relief as to get killed where we were. He said, "Varnum, you are a very uncomfortable companion." I left him.

Weir came to me afterwards & said Reno would let me send scouts if they would go. I had only four left with me, White Swan, who was badly wounded, & Half-Yellow-Face, of the Crows, and Goose (also wounded) and Forked Horn of the Rees. After long talks they finally agreed to try to get out that night & Reno gave me notes to give them. They did not go, however, & I doubt if they tried.

---

[128] George M. McDermott, aka Michael Burke, was born in Galway, County Clare, Ireland. His first enlistment was in 1870, but deserted in 1871. He then re-enlisted under the name Michael Burke in 1872. Later he surrendered under an amnesty. He was 1st Sergeant of Co. A at the time of the Bear Paw Mountain fight (Nez Perce Campaign) where he was killed, 30 Sept. 1877. (Hammer, p. 48.)

Later in the afternoon of the 26th we noticed that groups of Indians assembled on the high points of hills down the river. Their attacks grew less frequent, and about sunset almost discontinued.

It was decided to change our defensive line so as to get away from the stench of dead animals and get nearer water. This was gradually accomplished after dark. The up-stream defenses formed the down-stream line after the change, and we also extended a line down towards the river.

Fred Gerard and one of the Jackson boys (half-breed scout) came into our lines, and about midnight Lt. De Rudio and Private O'Neil came in.

Somehow it seemed to be in the air that the Indians had left and that relief was approaching. We knew that there was an expedition in the field under General Crook, and it seemed to me that this was the command most of us looked for. Trumpets were sounded at intervals to attract attention of any nearby troops. That Custer had been driven off and joined Terry & was approaching was also thought of & discussed.

I got a little sleep towards morning, but was up and around all the lines by daylight. There was no attack made on us. We had our horses watered during the night, sending small parties down to the river at a time. Having water, we got a breakfast, the first I had eaten since the morning of the 24th.

About 9 o'clock I think, dust was seen down the valley and from its regular formation we soon made out a Cavalry column. Lts. Wallace & Hare & possibly others, rode down the valley to meet them. It was Genl. Terry with four troops of the 2d Cavalry and six companies of the 7th Infantry.

I, Varnum

[Page or pages missing, and then continues]:
friends so as to recognize them. This work finished we marched to Terry's camp, and there, by night marches, to the mouth of the Little Big Horn on the Big Horn.

Capt. Grant Marsh, with the steamboat, *Far West,* was there & we embarked our wounded & sent them to Fort A. Lincoln.

A long campaign followed this, but nothing was accomplished, and we returned to Fort A. Lincoln in Sept., I think.

The cause of the massacre, seems to me, that the General divided his command in attacking an enemy many times as large as his own. In my

[*The narrative never completed*]

Appendices

Appendix A

Chronological Outline of the Life of
Charles Albert Varnum, 1849-1936
Army Service # o 13168
Compiled by Charles K. Mills, Tucson, Arizona

1849– 21 June: Born in Troy, New York
 Parents: John (b. 1823) & Nancy E. (Green) Varnum; married
  10 Apr. 1846
 Grandparents: Prescot (b. 1796) & Lydia Varnum
 Great-grandparens: Prescot & Elizabeth Varnum
 Lived in Dracut, Massachusetts; Pensacola & Tallahassee, Florida
1866– 18 August: Paymaster's clerk, US Navy until 31 March 1867
1868– 1 September: Entered West Point
 Room mate of George Daniel "Nick" Wallace, So. Carolina

★ ★ ★

7TH CAVALRY (1872-1904)

1872– 14 June: Graduation from West Point 17/57; appointed 2 Lt.
 7th Cavalry
 27 July: Assigned to Company A (vice Gibson promoted)
 1 October: Joined 7th Cavalry; remained DS at Huntsville, Ala.
1873– 31 January: Joined Company A at Elizabethtown
 6 March: Departed Louisville for Dakota Territory
 2 April: Arrived Yankton, D. T.
 10 June: Departed Fort Abraham Lincoln, D. T. for Stanley's
  Yellowstone Expedition
 4 August: First engagement with Sioux; commanded left of line
 11 August: Commanded sharpshooters in larger engagement with
  Sioux; commended in official report by Lt. Col. G. A. Custer
 22 September: Arrived Fort Lincoln
1874– 2 July: Participated in Custer's Black Hills Expedition; returned to Ft. Lincoln on 30 August 1874
 27 September: Departed Ft. Lincoln (with Co. A) for Livingston,
  Ala.; arrived 10 October 1874; made post quartermaster
1875– 2 February: Leave of absence until 2 March 1875
 18 May: Departed Livingston for Fort Randall, D.T.

26 July: Field duty in Black Hills evicting trespassers until 17 September 1875

3 November: Leave of absence until 12 April 1876

1876– 26 April: Arrived Lincoln; commenced recruiting Ree scouts for campaign

11 May: Departed Lincoln with 7th Cavalry; commanding detachment of Indian scouts

25 June: Battle of Little Big Horn; promoted to 1 Lt. (vice Calhoun killed); given command of provisional company & detachment of Indian scouts

26 September: Returned to Lincoln; re-assigned to Co. C (Capt. Henry Jackson & 2 Lt. Horatio G. Sickel); involved in brawl with Maj. Reno

1 October: Sent TDY to Co. I as acting company commander

20 October: Made acting regimental QM (vice Edgerly resigned)

14 November: Made regimental QM

1877– 13 September: Battle of Canyon Creek

30 September: Battle in Bear Paw Mountains
Spent balance of year in the field; based at Lincoln, spent most of following year (1878) in the field: August – Camp J. G. Sturgis, October – Camp Sheridan, Nebr., etc.

1878– 20 November: Returned to Lincoln

1879– 9 January: Sent on DS – Chicago for Reno Court of Inquiry

10 July: transferred (with regimental Hdq.) to Fort Meade, D.T.

31 October: Relieved of RQM by William H. Baldwin; made post adjutant of Ft. Lincoln

1880– 9 April: Assigned to Co. H (vice Gibson promoted)
Returned to Meade; Co. H with Capt. Frederick W. Benteen and 2 Lt. Albert J. Russell

4 September: Leave of absence – extended through 31 January 1881

1881– 1 February: on DS – Ft. Lincoln until 27 May 1881

1 June: Assumed command of Co. H (Benteen on DS – New York)

1882– 1 January: 2 Lt. Russell replaced by 2 Lt. Baldwin

6 April: Leave of absence until 20 April 1882

1883– 3 February: Relieved of command of H Troop by Capt. Edward G. Mathey until 23 May 1883

29 June: On DS – Pierre, D.T. until 17 July 1883

25 December: On leave of absence until 14 April 1884

1884– 26 April: On DS – locating wagon road to Dickinson, D.T. until 10 July 1884

16 September: Assumed command of H Troop in absence (on re-

cruiting service) of Capt. C.C. DeRudio; brief periods of DS
with 2 Lt. Baldwin assuming command; "in arrest" 22 April -
25 June 1886 at Ft. Meade; transferred H Troop to Ft. Yates,
October 1886

1886– 29 October: Relieved of command by Capt. DeRudio at Ft.
Yates

22 November: On DS – St. Paul (Dept. of Dakota Hdq.) until
7 December 1886

1887– 26 April: On DS – field, commanding detachment of Indian
scouts until 12 May 1887

10 July: On DS – field, commanding detachment of Indian scouts
until 5 August 1887

1888– 1 May: Re-assigned (with H Troop) to Ft. Meade; made
preparations to move to Ft. Sill, I.T.; led a battalion on the
march to Sill

1 August: Arrived at Ft. Sill, I.T.; made post QM until 31 March
1890; made post ADJ until 19 June 1890

1890– 19 June: Departed Ft. Sill for Ft. Riley; on leave ostensibly,
but Capt. McDougall (B Trp.) due to retire 22 July 1890

22 July: promoted to Capt. (vice McDougall retired)

4 August: Assumed command of B Troop at Riley as Captain
B Troop: 1 Lt. John C. Gresham & 2 Lt. Edwin C. Bullock

29 December: Battle of Wounded Knee

30 December: Battle of White Clay Creek (Drexel Mission)

1891– 26 February: Sick until 20 March 1891

1 July: 2 Lt. Robert J. Fleming (USMA '91) joined B Trp., re-
placing 2 Lt. Bullock

1892– 1 October: B Troop assigned to Ft. Sheridan, Ill.

Note: B Troop remained at Sheridan until 12 April 1896, when it
was transferred to Ft. Grant, Ariz. Terr.; in September of 1898,
B Troop was transferred to Ft. Sill; Varnum left Sheridan 5 July
1895 and did not rejoin until Ft. Sill in September 1898; B Troop
was commanded in his absence by 1 Lt. Selah R.H. Tompkins who
had joined at Sheridan in January of 1893

1895– 16 September: Arrived at Laramie as Professor of Military
Science at University of Wyoming

1897– 22 September: Awarded Medal of Honor for White Clay
Creek

1898– 30 August: Departed Laramie to rejoin B Troop at Ft. Sill,
preparatory to deployment to Cuba; B Troop: 1 Lt. Selah R.H.
Tompkins (since January 1893) & 2 Lt. Roy B. Harper,
USMA '97 (since May 1898)

I, Varnum

1899– 25 January: Arrived (commanding 2d Squadron 7th Cavalry) at Marianas, Cuba; re-assigned to 1st Squadron commanded by Maj. Edward M. Hayes at Camp Columbia – later Columbia Barracks, Havana, Cuba

2 May: Convoyed discharged soldiers to New York

9 June: Sent to hospital at Ft. McPherson, Ga.

15 July: As 1 Lt. Tompkins had been promoted to Capt. cmdg. M Troop in March, leaving 2 Lt. Harper in command of B Trp. alone since May, 1 Lt. William T. Littebrandt was assigned to command of B Trp. at Columbia Barracks

24 October: Varnum on medical leave of absence in Washington until 9 May 1900

1900– 19 May: Assigned as Assistant Adjutant General, Dept. of Colorado (Denver)

1901– 2 February: Promoted to Major, 7th Cavalry; remained on DS - Denver; balance of 7th Cavalry was still in Cuba, commanded by Col. Theodore C. Baldwin and Lt. Col. W. S. Edgerly; senior majors: Edwin A. Godwin and George F. Chase

1903– 31 May: Maj. Varnum rejoined 7th Cavalry at Camp Thomas, Ga. 7th Cav.: Col. Charles Morton (USMA '69) – since April 1903; Lt. Col. Samuel L. Woodward – since February 1903; Maj. Charles A. Varnum – since February 1901; Maj. Ezra B. Fuller – since October 1902; Maj. Loyd S. McCormick – since April 1903

23 December: Varnum commanded Camp Thomas *and* 7th Cav. regiment until 6 January 1904

1904– 24 April: commanded A, B and G Troops at Waco, Ga. until 30 June 1904

4 July: Re-assigned to Camp Thomas, Ga.

7th Cav.: Col. Charles Morton – since April 1903; Lt. Col. Daniel C. Pearson (USMA '70) – since July 1904; Maj. Charles A. Varnum – since February 1901; Maj. William J. Nicholson – since July 1904; Maj. Edwin P. Brewer – since September 1904

★   ★   ★

9TH CAVALRY (1904-1905)

1904– 22 September: Re-assigned to 9th (Negro) Cavalry; commanded by Col. Edward Godfrey & Lt. Col. Edwin A. Godwin – both ex-7th Cav. men, and stationed at Walla Walla, Wash.

6 October: Varnum arrived at Ft. Walla Walla

27 October: preceded regimental change of station, arriving at Ft. Riley

19 November: balance of 9th Cavalry arrived at Ft. Riley
1905– 10 April: effective date of promotion to Lt. Colonel, Cavalry
20 May: Departed Ft. Riley for 4th Cavalry (stationed at Ft. Walla Walla)

★ ★ ★
4TH CAVALRY (1905-1907)

1905– 4 June: Joined 4th Cavalry at Ft. Walla Walla, Wash.
4th Cav.: Col. Edgar Z. Steever (USMA '71); Lt. Col. Charles A. Varnum; Maj. James Lockett; Maj. Elon F. Wilcox; Maj. Frank A. Edwards
1 July: Entire regiment transferred to Presidio, San Francisco
26 August: Varnum on leave of absence until 4 September 1905
5 September: Commanded 2d Squadron 4th Cav. aboard transport *J. Buford* enroute to Philippines until arrival, 11 October
11 October: Arrived at Malabang, Mindanao, P.I.
20 December: Commanded post at Malabang until 20 December 1906
1906– 20 December: Commanded Camp Overton with balance of 4th Cav. on Jolo until 1 March 1907
1907– 1 March: Commanded post at Malabang until 28 June 1907
28 June: Enroute to USA
20 August: On DS – commanding Dept. of Dakota, St. Paul
14 September: Leave of absence until 5 November 1907
31 October: Date retirement from Regular Army for disability took effect; Varnum was on leave between assignments at this time

★ ★ ★
"RETIRED" (1907-1919)

1907– 16 November: Advisor to Militia, National Guard; later, of Idaho (Boise) until 10 October 1908
Note: Varnum was technically retired, but only from the Regular Army List; he remained on active duty as a "retired" Regular Lt. Col., with full rank, pay, privileges, etc.
1908– November: Assigned as Professor of Military Science at University of Maine, remaining there until June 1912
1912– 1 July: Recruiting duty at Portland, Ore. until 20 Feb. 1917
1917– 1 March: Recruiting duty, Kansas City, Mo. until 16 Sept. 1918
1918– 9 July: Promoted to Colonel ("Retired" Regular Army)
1 October: Made disbursing officer at Ft. Mason (Presidio) San Francisco

I, Varnum

1919– 8 April: Relieved from active duty

★　　　　　★　　　　　★

1936– 26 February: Died at Letterman General Hospital, Presidio, San Francisco

28 February: Funeral at New Post Chapel; interment at National Cemetery

Appendix B

Testimony of Charles A. Varnum
at the Reno Court of Inquiry

After the Battle of the Little Big Horn, there was much pressure exerted upon Major Reno from Frederick Whittaker, Mrs. Custer and others in the Custer camp; Major Reno was under attack for his lack of military expertise and gumption. Finally, unable to bear this burden any longer, Major Reno requested a Court of Inquiry to look into his conduct at that battle. Reno was damned with faint praise, and indeed, the officers of the 7th U. S. Cavalry joined forces and presented a united front for "the good of the regiment."

The Court of Inquiry convened at Chicago on 13 January 1879. Twenty-three officers and civilians testified at that Inquiry; First Lieutenant Charles A. Varnum was the fourth to testify. His testimony is included here as part of the profile being created.

The Reno Court of Inquiry is perhaps the single most important document extant on the controversial "Custer's Last Stand." In many respects it created as much controversy as it buried. A very few copies of this document exist for general readership, but to ignore it for that reason is to be remiss as a student of the story.

In the final analysis, Major Reno was found not wanting and as a consequence no General Court Martial was ordered. I personally believe that today, given the knowledge of the subject now known, it would be a different story.

Varnum's testimony was spread over three days, January 21-23, 1879, the eighth to tenth days of the Inquiry. Present on each day were the officers of the Court, Colonels John H. King, 9th Infantry, Wesley Merritt, 5th Cavalry, Lieutenant Colonel W. B. Royall, 3rd Cavalry, and Recorder First Lieutenant Jesse M. Lee, Adjutant, 9th Infantry. Also present, of course, were Major Reno and counsel. First Lieutenant Charles A. Varnum was called to the stand . . .

Lieut. Charles A. Varnum, 7th Cavalry, a witness called by the Recorder, being first duly sworn, to testify the truth, the whole truth and nothing but the truth, testified as follows:

I, Varnum

Q. State your name, rank, regiment, and where serving.

A. Charles A. Varnum, 1st Lieut. and Q. M. 7th Cavalry, serving at Fort A. Lincoln, D.T.

Q. On what duty were you on the 25th and 26th days of June, 1876, and with what command?

A. I was second lieutenant, 7th Cavalry at that time, in command of a detachment of Indian scouts, with the 7th Cavalry under Gen. Custer in the vicinity of the Little Big Horn river, Montana Territory.

Q. Of what troops or companies did Gen. Custer's command consist on the morning of June 25, 1876?

A. It consisted of twelve companies of the 7th Cavalry, and a detachment of Indian scouts which I commanded.

Q. Was Major Reno, 7th Cavalry with that command?

A. He was, as second in command.

Q. Against what enemy if any was that command operating?

A. Against the hostile Sioux Indians.

Q. State whether or not the twelve companies of the 7th Cavalry were together on the morning of the 25th of June, 1876.

A. They were.

Q. At that time what were the indications if any of the proximity of hostile Indians?

A. I was not on the trail exactly on the morning of the 25th, but was detached scouting. The indications were the statements of our Indians that they could see the village.

Q. State if you know into what battalions the command was divided on the 25th of June and what officers were assigned to the command of those battalions.

A. I was not present with the command when the division was made and do not know, except as appeared after.

Q. State whether or not Major Reno had command of a separate battalion on the 25th of June.

A. He had.

Q. How many companies were in his battalion and what was its effective strength?

A. I don't know what command was assigned to Major Reno. I only know what was under his command when I met him. He then had three companies with him. The number of men is a matter of opinion only. I think the companies averaged about forty men each.

Q. Do you know what orders were given by Gen. Custer or his adjutant to Major Reno on the 25th of June, 1876, with reference to attacking or pursuing the hostile Indians?

A. I did not hear any; I was not present.

Q. Was there any separation of the command, and at what point did the separation of Major Reno's command from Gen. Custer occur?

A. The command of Major Reno was passing Gen. Custer and his staff at the time I reported to Gen. Custer. That was about a mile from where Major Reno afterwards crossed the Little Big Horn. I started on and fell in with the command as it went. I think one company of the battalion had crossed the river when I reached it.

Q. Describe with as much particularity as you can the movements of the three companies of Major

Reno's command, from the time it separated from Gen. Custer's column, to the time those companies came within sight of the Indian village or within sight of the Indians, and state what orders if any were given by Major Reno during that particular period of time.

A. I do not know whether the Indians had been seen by Major Reno's command at the time it separated from Gen. Custer or not. I had seen the Indians in the bottom for an hour or more before the separation took place, as I was on the high bluffs. The three companies moved out in column of fours at a rapid gait. I rode at the flank at a rapid gait to overtake the head of the column, crossing the river as I have stated.

Q. After separating from Gen. Custer's column, where did you last see it before crossing the river?

A. I did not see it again after I left it. Probably I might have seen it but I did not look for it.

Q. When Major Reno's command went down to this ford how far was it ahead of Gen. Custer's column at the time it reached the ford, judging by the gait both were going?

A. When I left Gen. Custer he was at the head of his column moving at a walk. Major Reno pulled out at a trot. From what I have seen of the country since, Gen. Custer must have turned off so that it is impossible for me to tell what was their relative positions. They may have been travelling in the same general direction or not, I don't know.

Q. What time of day was it when the village was first seen by you, and how far was Major Reno's command from the village and how far was Gen. Custer's column from it?

A. I had seen the village before the command separated.

Q. Describe fully and clearly the location of the village when it was seen by you; the topography of the country around it in reference to the stream, the hills and mountains around it, as it appeared at the time or as subsequently ascertained by you.

A. The village was situated along the left bank of the Little Big Horn, and owing to the lay of the land, that is the bends of the stream, and the timber around on the left bank it was impossible unless you get out on the plain to see much of the village. I could see some of the teepees but it was impossible to see the whole extent of it; and never having been over the ground since where the village stood I don't know the lay of the country there.

Q. From the view you had of the village or of the Indians, what was your opinon at the time as to the size of the village; that is, the effective fighting force and state to what extent those impressions were confirmed by events that transpired after?

A. I don't think I ever made an estimate of the strength of the Indians till it was over. There were more Indians than I ever saw before. I had seen immense numbers of Indians from the top of the bluffs while out scouting and knew there was a very large village there.

Q. Begin at the right bank of the Little Big Horn, where Major Reno separated from Gen. Custer, and give a detailed description, in narrative form, of the successive movements of Major Reno's column; the orders given by Major Reno or executed under his direction, stating every circumstance within your knowledge as to his conduct as the commander of troops up to and including the 26th of June, 1876. In answer to this question give a description of the ground passed over by Major Reno's command, the stream or streams crossed, the engagements had, and in short, every circumstance having any relation to the conduct of Major Reno or his command on the 25th or 26th days of June, 1876.

A. As I said before, I left the head of Gen. Custer's column to overtake the battalion that was passing us to get ahead of the troops themselves to scout again and the head of the column soon after crossed a little tributary of the Little Big Horn. I was about the middle of the column as it passed there and I was forced off the trail and didn't join the command until it was just crossing that ford. One company had got across the ford at the time I got across myself. There were eight or ten Indian scouts with me at the time, and as soon as the column passed I was joined by Lieut. Hare, who had been detailed to assist me in scouting. He started out fifty to seventy-five yards ahead of the command. The bottom was opened out wider as we went down the stream. There was quite a large body of the Indians some little distance off, and they were running away from us and then running back, running back and forth across the prairie and toward us, and in every direction, apparently trying to kick up all the dust they could, and it was so covered with dust it was impossible to discover the number of Indians there. At times they were apparently running away from us and then halting and circling around and making a heavy dust. I

noticed all of a sudden that they stopped and
turned backward, and I turned my head around
and glanced back to see the cause, and I noticed a
battalion deploying from column into line, and
I supposed at the time that they supposed they were
going to halt, and turned back on us at that time.
The command then moved forward again in line
and we rode on, I suppose, fifty yards in front of
the line, and as we went down the bottom we
worked out toward the bluffs, toward the left of
Col. Reno's line. The Indians let us come closer
and closer as we came down, and we could see
about half way down to where the final halt was
made, and we could see quite a number of teepees,
and they evidently were circling amongst themselves, and when they got down opposite the village they didn't uncover the village much. We
went on down possibly two miles and the line
halted and dismounted. I was not present and
didn't hear any of the orders, and don't know what
orders were given. When the line halted, I rode
with Lieut. Hare, in toward the line, and the
Indian scouts, as they generally fight in the Indian fashion were gone I don't know where, and
my old company that I belonged to was in the line,
Captain Moylan's, and I went back and reported
to him and told him I should stop with his company during the fight. The line was then deployed
perpendicularly to the general direction of the
river, and the skirmish immediately commenced
between the Indians and the troops. When I had
been on the line ten or fifteen minutes I heard
somebody say that "G" company was going to

charge a portion of the village down through the
woods, or something to that effect. I heard some
of the men calling out "G" company is going to
"charge!" I was on my horse and I rode down into
the timber to go with the company that was going
to charge the village. In the timber there is a little
glade or opening, and I know in riding in on to
this opening I could see the stream in one direction, so we must have been near the stream, and I
could see the line of the opening in front, and
supposed there was a detached portion of the village on the other side of the stream, and that is
where they were going. I heard no orders. It was
just a rumor that I followed, and I saw Col. Reno
there. He was right with "G" company, evidently
deploying it, or assisting to deploy it to go through
the woods. The company was on the downstream
side of the opening and I said: "I am going to
charge!" or something like that, and I rode to
where the Colonel was, and the colonel asked me
if I had just come from the line in front, and I
told him I had a few moments ago. In coming
down there I was delayed by the narrow intricate
paths in the first edge of the timber getting through
there with my horse, and he said: "I wish you
would go back there, and see how things are going
on, and come back and report to me." I turned
back on my horse, and was riding across this opening when I met Lieut. Hodgson and asked him if
he had just come from the line, and he said he
had, and I told him Major Reno wanted to know
what was going on on the line, and if he would
report to him, I would ride up and come down

again a few moments afterward. I was with him
a few minutes afterward. He thought his horse
was shot, and he was anxious to know about it, and
that delayed me a minute, then I went upon the
line. I went up through the paths to where the line
was. The line at that time appeared to have fallen
back to the edge of the timber, that is, it was lying
on the edge of the timber instead of being perpendicular to it. The command was lying in the timber, and I could not see all of the men. I saw Captain Moylan the first when I got onto the edge of
the line, and he called out — I don't know that he
intended to speak to me — that the horses that we
had dismounted from were beyond the left flank
of our line, that the Indians were circling into the
timber toward his left flank, and would cut off our
horses, and that all our extra ammunition was
there, and that something must be done. I told him
that I would bring them up, and I went back. In
order to go down the line, I had to go down into
the woods to this opening, and I rode down to the
left of the line, and calling out for "A" company
men to follow me with their horses. I went up with
my own company, and we came right in the rear
of where Captain Moylan was. This was about at
the rear of his own line. I dismounted then, and
went up on the line, and as I did so I heard Captain Moylan call that his men were out of ammunition; and he ordered that each alternate man
should fall back from the line and get ammunition
out of their saddlebags, and return to the line, so
as to let the others go back and get ammunition
from their saddlebags. Then I got up to the right

of the line and met Mr. Girard and Charley Reynolds, and stopped and talked with them I guess
about a minute or two or three minutes. When I
heard from the woods cries of "Charge! Charge!
We are going to charge!" There was quite a con-
fusion, – something about a charge down in the
woods, and I jumped up and said: "What's that?"
and started down into the woods and grabbed my
horse. Everybody was mounted. I didn't hear any
orders. I just understood the men calling that they
were going to charge, and I grabbed my horse and
mounted him, and this being in the bushes and
the men mounting just outside of the bushes kept
me in and I couldn't get out until the men had
passed. As soon as they passed so that I could get
out I got into the path myself and came out with
the men. The head of the column was then about
a couple of rods or something like that from the
edge of the timber as I came out and I let my horse
have his head and pretty soon overtook the head
of the column. I had a very fast horse. As I came
up with the head of the column it was probably
about half way from there to the ford at which we
crossed soon after. I came upon the left hand side
of the column, and I didn't see any officer at the
head – that is, as I came up, understand. I supposed there had been a charge started, and that the
first men out of the woods had struck some Indians
and wheeled and started for those, and the others
might have followed them. I didn't know what
was up, and I yelled to them first to stop, and my
horse was plunging and I plunged by, and I saw
Major Reno and Captain Moylan. Not seeing

the command at all on the left, I supposed they were not there; and then they went on from there to the river and crossed the stream. Immediately on the other bank of the stream is a very high bluff, that went up probably, I should judge, one-third of the way, as I remember it now, and I know that the horses were pretty well played out. They were all panting, and climbing that perfectly steep hill, they could hardly make it. I don't know exactly what did happen at that time at the head of the column, because my orderly that had been with me was very badly shot, and his horse was shot, and his horse fell with him there, and I stopped to pick up a loose horse and mount my orderly. The head of the column halted there, or there was a sort of a delay there, and somebody said they were going to move up on the the hill, and there was no use of stopping there; so we went up to the top of the hill.

When we arrived on the top of the hill I found there were several men wounded there, and two or three of them were of my old company, the first sergeant and one or two others, and I stopped with them for two or three minutes, getting them off their horses. A few moments afterward a column of troops was in sight coming down the stream toward us, and we stopped there until they came up, which was probably ten or fifteen minutes. My statements in regard to time are more or less a guess. In ten or fifteen minutes Col. Benteen came up with his command of three companies. At that time a great number of the men had been in the saddle I suppose for a long time,

and they took their canteens and ran right down
to the stream to get some water. I don't recollect
seeing Col. Reno there. We were all about there.
I don't remember him exactly until he came up
from the river. He had been down to the river,
and when he came up from the river he spoke
about finding Lieut. Hodgson's body at the foot
of the bluffs, and that his watch was gone, but that
he had some remaining little trinkets that were
on Lieut. Hodgson's body. At this time I don't
think that Captain McDougall's company with
the packs was in sight. I may be mistaken about
it, but I don't think he was, as I remember that
Lieut. Hare started out soon afterward to go and
hurry them up. We waited there then for five or
ten minutes, when Col. Reno told me to take a
detachment and go down and bury Lieut. Hodgson's body. There was nothing there to bury it with,
and I told him I would have to wait until the
packs came up. We remained there until the packs
came up, about three-quarters of an hour afterward. I then got two spades from the packs and
started with about six men to go down to the river
and bury the bodies. About two-thirds of the way
down I saw a lot of men coming out of the woods,
and I stopped to see what was up.

There was a citizen and quite a number of soldiers who came from the woods dismounted and
were climbing the bluffs, coming up out of the
bottom. There was timber immediately in the
rear of where the fight had occured, down in the
bottom. As I started with the men to bury the
bodies, some body, I think, Lieut. Wallace, called

to me that they wanted me to come back, and I started then immediately up the hill. I got up the hill, and it was very hard, slow work – it was badlands there – and when I got up there most of the command had started on to move on down the stream along the bluffs, with the exception, I think, of Captain Moylan's company, and possibly some of the others. He had most of the wounded. I think they were all his company, and the men that he had left when he got out of the bottom were hardly sufficient to carry them. There were very few men there belonging to "A" company after the fight, and they moved very slowly. I stayed with him some time, and I think Captain McDougall's company, "B," sent a platoon to assist him in, carrying the wounded. I started along with "A" company for a while, and as that was near the river, I started up ahead again. I had no command at all. About a mile and a half from there I joined Captain Weir's company. That was on the far point of a long range of high bluffs which ran along the right bank of the Little Big Horn. I went on to where his company was dismounted and firing at the Indians, who seemed to be coming from out on the prairie and turning back. It was quite long range, but there was a good many shot being fired at him, and he was firing away – a slow fire – a shot now and then at quite a little distance. All the Indians in that country seemed to be coming a little distance off as fast as they could travel in that direction. Soon after this we turned and gradually dropped back. I didn't see the troops leave that farther point, but I went back to Captain Moylan and helped with the wounded a little while. I rode back slowly to the rear, and the troops gradually fell back to a point, I think, a little farther up the stream than where we touched the bluffs. It was quite a slow movement, as one or two of the companies were dismounted. They got their horses and fell into line, and dropped back into the position that was selected and one which we afterward fought.

The firing was kept up. The entire force seemed to have turned back against us, and we had to fight falling back dismounted to cover the retreat on to the position where we were located afterward. The firing was kept up as long as we could see, until night – a very heavy firing on us, and the men fortified as well as they could with the tin-cups and sabres and the next day we continued to fight nearly all day, and the day following was joined by Gen. Terry.

Q. State if you know at what hour of the day Major Reno's command separated from Gen. Custer's column to go across the ford.

A. Any statement I may make in regard to time would be a guess on my part. The last time I know anything about was eight o'clock that morning. I was then on top of the mountain, having been sent there the night before. I have very little to base an opinion of time upon unless I connect it with someone's else's statement. I have thought of it a great deal, and I think it must have been two o'clock. I base my opinion a good deal on other people's opinions, compared with my own as to time.

Q. Can you locate the time with reference to any particular object; a knoll or teepee?

A. The separation must have occurred soon after we passed a teepee which stood on a tributary of the Little Big Horn.

Q. State if you can how long it was after the separation till Major Reno had effected a crossing of the river.

A. Probably ten or fifteen minutes.

Q. Had the whole command got over in that time?

A. Yes sir, I think so – in fifteen minutes.

Q. State whether there was any delay at the crossing or in the crossing; if so how much and for what purpose?

A. I don't know about any delay. The water was quite deep there and the river was probably twenty-five or thirty feet wide, and in a column of troops getting across there is necessarily some delay, they can't keep closed up in the water. How much of a stoppage I can't say.

Q. Did you notice that any of them stopped to water their horses, or anything of that kind?

A. No sir, everything seemed to be moving rapidly.

Q. State in what condition the men and horses were at that time as regards efficiency – whether the horses were comparatively fresh or entirely played out, or any facts about that matter and also about the men.

A. I had not ridden with the column since the morning of the 25th; I had been in the hills all the time. As for myself I was completely exhausted, and nothing but the excitement of going into action kept me in the saddle at all.

I, Varnum

Q. State what had brought on the exhaustion in your case.

A. It was riding thirty miles on the 24th, then being sent back ten miles, making fifty miles; then I rode twenty miles more that night and did not get to the point I was sent to till two o'clock in the morning; and as soon as Gen. Custer came up with the command I was in the saddle again. I was almost constantly in the saddle from five o'clock on the morning of the 24th except a short time on the morning of the 25th.

Q. State the relative distance you had travelled as compared with that of the command.

A. They had travelled about the same distance I had, except about twenty miles of the afternoon of the 24th, and the difference between going along on the trail and riding out on the hills.

Q. How far was the crossing where Major Reno's command crossed the river and the nearest part of the Indian village, as you observed it at the time or after?

A. I have always stated the distance to Major Reno's skirmish line was about two miles, as near as I could judge it, and from there it was about eight hundred yards to where the nearest teepees were in a bend of the river. Then the main bulk of the village was below that. There must have been quite a solid lot of teepees in that bend.

Q. Describe if you can, the route of the advance of Major Reno's command from the crossing, as compared with the course of the stream, up to where the men were dismounted and deployed as skirmishers.

A. They moved down the valley of the stream, following its general course; not a straight line but merely a direct course. The river is very crooked.

Q. After Major Reno's command crossed the river, how much time elapsed till they were halted and deployed as skirmishers?

A. Fifteen or twenty minutes I should think; maybe more or less.

Q. At what gait did the command travel across the bottom from the crossing to where the men were deployed as skirmishers?

A. I think at about a fast trot, I am not certain. I was moving ahead and did not notice that particularly. I was moving rapidly and they were close behind me.

Q. Did Major Reno's command encounter any opposition going from the crossing to where it was halted?

A. There was no absolute contact between his command and the Indians.

Q. State as near as you can, in reference to the point of time established in your own mind, at what time of day it was the men were deployed as skirmishers.

A. It must have been half past two o'clock. That is, assuming my other statement is about correct.

Q. What was the character of the ground from the right of Major Reno's command to the river at the time it was first deployed as skirmishers?

A. The timber was very heavy along the edge of what was called the second bench with dense undergrowth (underbrush), and little paths made by animals through it, then rather an open glade with grass in places, then flows the river, with small trees down near the river. That is as I noticed it at the time.

Q. About how far was it from the right of his line to the river?

A. I could not see through and don't know. It may have been a hundred yards.

Q. State whether or not Major Reno charged the enemy when he was within engaging distance, or did he at any time give such order, and if so was it obeyed?

A. I was not near enough to have heard the command if it was given, and can't say.

Q. When the command was halted were the Indians firing on it?

A. I believe a few shots had been fired before the command was deployed. There was a sort of engagement between the scouts and the Indians. I don't know who commenced the firing or where; I know there were some stray shots.

Q. Was that immediately before the command deployed, or about that time?

A. About that time.

Q. There was no firing by Indians on the line at the time the command was halted and deployed?

A. No sir, except those few shots, that I know of.

Q. Where were those few shots?

A. At the left toward the bluff. Lieut. Hare I think fired a few shots.

Q. Describe the nature of the ground in the immediate front of Major Reno's command when it was halted and deployed as skirmishers.

A. It was open prairie. I learned after that there were ravines beyond, but as far as I saw them it was open, the same as the bottom we had passed over.

Q. How long after Major Reno's command had been halted and deployed as skirmishers before any engagement began there – any firing of consequence?

A. They commenced firing as soon as they got in shape, both from the troops and the Indians.

Q. What advance, if any, was made by Major Reno's command after the engagement commenced?

A. There was no advance made that I know of.

Q. State as near as you can, the number of Indians that engaged Major Reno's command at that place, and whether during the engagement there was any increase or decrease in the number of Indians, and what movements if any were made by the Indians with reference to Major Reno's command at that place.

A. It is almost impossible to estimate the strength of mounted Indians. There was a very large force there soon after the command was dismounted, and there was a large force circling around us all the time, and passing around to the left and rear. I was on the line about fifteen minutes and then went into the timber as I stated before. When I came out I was only on the line three or four minutes and I did not pay very much attention to it. There was very heavy firing going on on both sides; I was lying in the edge of the woods with Girard and Reynolds and was anxious to get a drink out of Girard's flask, and was paying more attention to that than to the Indians.

Q. How far did the Indians seem to be away at that time?

A. The heaviest force of Indians was toward the

immediate right of the line as that covered the village. I think they were about three or four hundred yards from the line, and then there were others here and there running around at long range.

Q. About what number of Indians were in Major Reno's immediate front, firing on him when you were on the brow of the hill?

A. I don't believe there were less than three or four hundred, and there may have been a great many more.

Q. Before you left the line to go back into the woods as you have testified, how many Indians were engaging the line and at what distance from the line?

A. The number actually firing I can't say. It was very heavy fire coming from the Indians and up the valley; the whole valley seemed to be covered with them. How many Indians that dust covered it is impossible to estimate. That dust more or less covered the main force of the Indians. As a rule they fire from their horses and they were scampering around, pumping their Winchester rifles into us.

Q. How far was the dust from you so as to obscure the Indians?

A. The heavy dust was eight hundred or a thousand yards out.

Q. State how long the engagement lasted there from its commencement there in the woods till Major Reno's command fell back or left the woods.

A. I would estimate it at half an hour. That is a mere estimate.

Q. Up to the time the command left, state if you know, how many of Major Reno's command had been killed or disabled.

A. I know of the first sergeant of my company, and my orderly being shot. With the exception of those two I don't know.

Q. You were on the line before it went into the woods?

A. Yes sir.

Q. Did you see when there were any casualties?

A. No sir.

Q. Did you see any casualties on the line while on the brow of the hill?

A. If there had been any I would have not known it, because if any of the men had been shot they would have dropped into the woods and I would not see it.

Q. Did the first sergeant get the command up on the hill?

A. Yes sir. He may have got his wound about the time he started out, at any rate he came in on his horse. Nor do I know when Strobe (Strode) was shot.

Q. State if you know what cause led to the retreat of that command from the timber at that time?

A. I have stated all I know of the circumstances of their leaving. I don't know that I know anything beyond that.

Q. State whether or not there are trumpet or bugle calls for cavalry for assembly, advance, retreat, charge, etc.

A. Yes sir.

Q. Were any trumpet or bugle calls sounded from the

time Major Reno's command left that skirmish line during the 25th and 26th of June?

A. I do not recollect any bugle calls till the evening of the 26th.

Q. If there had been any would you have heard them?

A. Undoubtedly I should have heard them, but it is possible I might have heard them and not recollect it, but I don't think I heard any.

Q. Then state if you know in what way the order to charge or fall back or retreat, or what ever it was, was communicated to the command.

A. I have no idea whatever. I was on the line and heard some of the men yelling, "They are going to charge!" "They are going to charge!" or something like that, and I made for my horse and mounted it.

Q. State whether you felt at that time that the command was in any special or great danger, if so describe it.

A. It was not a very safe place. I don't exactly know how you mean. I only know what I have stated; I don't know anything special. I might say that at the time that movement was made a great many bullets had commenced to drop into the woods from the rear. I did not see any Indians there, and whether the bullets were from the bluffs above or from below I don't know. The bottom near the stream was heavy underbrush.

Q. Were those shots high or low?

A. Shots coming into the woods it is difficult to tell. I could hear the bullets chip the trees as they would strike, but from where they were coming I did not determine because there was a heavy fire in front.

Q. Do you know whether or not any effort was made to ascertain where that fire from the rear came from?

A. I don't know about that.

Q. Do you know whether any attempt was made to dislodge them from that position?

A. My first knowledge of any firing from that direction was just before we left.

Q. State if you know whether either at the time that command left the woods or on its way to the crossing of the river, there was any point designated for the command to rally or retreat to, and if so state who designated it.

A. I don't know of any.

Q. How far was the point to which Major Reno's command retreated from the river, where he crossed it on the retreat?

A. Probably about four hundred yards in a straight line, up a steep hill.

Q. How far was the crossing from where the command was stationed in the woods?

A. About three-fourths of a mile.

Q. From the time the head of the column left the woods on that retreat or charge about how long did it take the troops to reach that crossing?

A. Assuming my estimate of the distance is correct, they were not more than six or eight minutes.

Q. When the command left the woods what number of Indians did you see in the immediate front of Major Reno's command while the command was going to the crossing?

A. As I said before the heaviest force of Indians was covering their village. When we came out I was not at the head of the column, and have no idea how many Indians were in front. When I came out there were a good many Indians scampering along with their Winchester rifles across their saddles firing into the column. As I came down there is a sharp bend in the river and there were a good many in there next to the river. I soon got to the head of the column, probably about half way to the crossing, and by the time I got there, the Indians in our front had run off.

Q. When you started to go out of the timber how many Indians did you see to your left?

A. Probably fifteen or twenty, maybe more. And on that point of land about half way from the skirmish line to the crossing there were some clumps of bushes and there were Indians running around in there. I have understood since there were several bodies found near there.

Q. Did the command make any halts on crossing the creek to succor the wounded or drive the Indians?

A. There was no halt made till we were across the river.

Q. Did the command on its retreat engage the Indians, or was the command engaged in firing at them?

A. A great many of the men were using their revolvers.

Q. Describe the manner of getting into the river.

A. There was only one way to get in and that was to jump in. It was a straight bank. The other side was a little better, but my horse nearly threw me as he jumped up on the other side.

Q. State if any of the men or horses fell back into the river there.

A. I only know from hearsay.

Q. How near to the river did the Indians pursue the command there?

A. I can't say. When I got across, I started up a ridge to the left of the command and some of the men called to me to come back, and I came back. Evidently they saw Indians I did not see, because Dr. De Wolf started up that same ridge and was shot. When I got to the column I found my orderly, Strode, wounded and I stopped to assist him, and did not notice what was behind.

Q. State whether or not that crossing was covered during the retreat.

A. Not that I know of. I know of no deployment to cover it. About the time the greater part of the command had crossed there was but few shots around us, no heavy firing at all, except the instances I have related, and, I think there was another man killed there, a corporal of company "A" was killed there and another man near Dr. De Wolf.

Q. Was that at the time of crossing or after?

A. After we crossed; that firing must have come from the hill above us. I know Dr. De Wolf was shot from the hill above us.

Q. There were Indians on the hill in the position you were going to?

A. Yes sir.

Q. What is the formation for a charge of cavalry?

A. That depends on what you are going to charge. The battalion might have charged drawn up in a line or drawn up in a column of fours, depending on what the object of the charge is. If there was a charge to pass through a body of Indians I think in a column of fours would be a good formation with the number of men at his disposal. That would give the men an opportunity to use their revolvers – they could not use their carbines.

Q. With a large force of Indians in front, would that be a good formation to pass through them?

A. That would depend on the number of men; I would not like to string out a regiment in that way.

Q. How did the command go across the bottom on the retreat?

A. I think from what I saw it was started in a column of fours. But take a lot of horses many of which had not been drilled before as ours were and form a charge in column of fours and by the time you go a hundred yards the men will not all be in their places.

Q. Describe the gait at which Major Reno's command went across the bottom.

A. It was a good fast gallop. I don't think the head of the column was making as fast as it could. I was not long in getting to the head of the column, and I had to saw on my horse's mouth to keep him down to the gait they were travelling, but I had a good horse.

Q. Was your horse excited at the time?

A. If he got a chance to run he was generally excited.

Q. When you saw the command going across the bottom how did it impress you, as a flight, a retreat or a charge?

A. When I started out of the woods I did not know what was up. I had heard talk of charge. My impression at first was that they were going to charge somewhere, but seeing no officer as I got to the head of the column, I spoke to some of the men to know what was up, but just then I saw the commanding officer, and said no more.

Q.   Give as careful a description as you can of the stream where Major Reno's command crossed it on the retreat, as to its width, depth of water, banks on either side and as to its practicability as a crossing.

A.   There were about four and one-half feet of water in the stream. The banks were probably four or five feet high; the stream was probably twenty feet wide. The time I passed over it with those troops was the only time I was at it, but that is my recollection now.

Q.   From the time you joined the head of the command going to that crossing were there any Indians between the command and the crossing?

A.   I did not see any.

Q.   Were there any immediately to the right or left?

A.   There may have been to the right, I don't know. I did not see any to the left, after passing that point I have indicated.

Q.   Were you in position to have seen them if they had been there?

A.   If they were to the left, yes. If they had been to the right I might not have noticed them.

Q.   If they had been within a hundred yards of the right would you have not noticed them?

A.   I might not unless they had killed or wounded someone. I don't think they followed us to the river. That is they were not at the head of the column.

Q.   From the time the command reached the crossing

on its retreat till it got on the hill what was its condition; was it cool, calm and easily handled or otherwise?

A. Everybody I saw was considerably excited. They were considerably excited when they went in, for that matter.

Q. State as a matter of fact whether the command was in a condition to be handled; whether the men seemed to have any confidence or not.

A. It is difficult for me to state anything about that, because for a long time before that I had not served with the command and knew but a few men even of my own company. I had been detached and absent a long time.

Q. Was the command demoralized to any degree when it reached the top of the hill?

A. It was demoralized to a certain degree. They had left a great many behind them. The organization was not as good as when it went in there. A great many men were gone from the organization.

Then at two o'clock P.M. the Court adjourned to meet at eleven A.M., tomorrow, Wednesday, Jany. 22, 1879.

[Ninth Day.] The examination of Lieut. Varnum by the Recorder, was continued as follows:

Q. Describe as near as you can, the point to which Major Reno's command retreated across the river, to the top of the hill. State its adaptability as a defensible position, before the arrival of Captain Benteen's column.

A. The position was immediately on top of the high bluffs, and must be pretty near the position on which we afterward fought. I can't state whether

it was such as would have been within range of
higher points. I think it was a very good defensible position.

Q. How high was that point above the level of the
water there?

A. I judge about one hundred feet high.

Q. State how it occurred that the men were halted
or rallied at that point – who stopped the men
there?

A. I don't know.

Q. Were you there?

A. Yes sir.

Q. Were you there when the men were coming up
the hill?

A. I don't remember what time I got on top of the
hill. I stopped on the side of the hill a while with
the wounded men, and whether I got up with the
head or the rear of the column, I don't recollect.

Q. At the time you stopped on the side of the hill was
there any halt of the command, or did it go past
you?

A. The command stopped there, and I am pretty
certain it was Major Reno said that place at the
side hill was no place to form at, we had better
go to the top of the hill. I was talking to Captain
Moylan, and I am not certain whether it was he
or Major Reno said that.

Q. State whether there was any point or place on the
left bank of the stream which, in your opinion as
an officer, could have been occupied by Major
Reno's command for defense or attack. If so describe that place or point with reference to the
position which was occupied by his command

where it engaged the Indians; whether it was the same place or some other place, this before the retreat began, and state fully the facts upon which your opinion on that matter is based, showing the practicability or impracticability of Major Reno's command remaining in or going to such place, either to defend himself against the Indians or to attack.

A. The position we were in in the timber was as good a place as any on the left bank of the stream, as far as I can judge now. I don't know much about the country up or down the stream from that. I don't know the size of that piece of timber, but it does not come to me that he had men enough to cover the entire position which he would necessarily have to cover to keep the Indians out of it. It does not seem to me now that he had men enough to hold that entire piece of timber.

Q. How did it seem to you at that time?

A. As far as the front of the line is concerned, on the second bench, at the edge of the timber, it was an excellent position to lay and fight the Indians. I did not go to the rear, and what advantages the Indians would have in coming into the timber on our rear, or what precautions it would be necessary to take to keep them out. I could not judge without seeing it.

Q. Was it a cut bank or a slope to the rear on the same side Major Reno's command was?

A. I don't know; I never was down to the river.

Q. You said you could see through and see where the river seemed to wind around. Was that below or above or to the right of Major Reno's position?

A. That was downstream from the open glade I spoke of.

Q. State whether the river in that direction came around his right flank or in that direction.

A. I don't know how far that bend makes, whether he could have run his line to the river or not.

Q. Did the river come in the vicinity of the right of his line as far as you saw it?

A. I only saw it diagonally to the right of company "G" and whether it actually came to the right of Major Reno's position or not, I don't know. There was dense timber there and I was not down in it.

Q. State whether that position in the timber threatened the village and to what extent and whether it would create a diversion and hold any number of Indians in his front.

A. Any body of men placed near an Indian village like that, is certainly threatening to the village. It certainly created a diversion to the extent of the number of Indians necessary to keep us in the woods. They were bound to have that number in front of us.

Q. How many did they keep as near as you can get at it?

A. I think from what I saw that the Indians were withdrawn from us very near the time we left the woods. I don't think there had been a great many withdrawn till we left. It seemed that whatever attack was made somewhere else, was made about the time we left the woods.

Q. State whether it seemed as though the entire force of the village was there in your immediate front, confronting Major Reno's command, up to about this time you speak of.

A. No sir, I don't think the entire force of the village was attacking us in the woods. I don't think the entire force of the Indians was ever attacking us because after we got on the hill we could see parties of Indians a long way off.

Q. I refer to the large mass of them.

A. I judge the main fighting force of the village was against us there after we dismounted. How many I can't estimate.

Q. State in your opinion as a military officer, when Major Reno's command had retreated from that place near the village as you have described, having the river between his commend and the village, from the position thus taken he was in a condition or situation to threaten the village or make any diversion against the Indians in support of any other attacking column; and state your grounds for such opinion.

A. As long as we remained at that position on the hill we were certainly in no position to threaten the village. We were out of range of it, and could certainly create no diversion while we were there.

Q. Was the command in any condition to create any diversion at that time?

A. No sir, it was not.

Q. State where you last saw Gen. Custer's column or any part of it. Describe that as fully as you can, either by the map or otherwise.

A. These bluffs on the map do not look right to me at all. At the time I saw the command I speak of I did not know it was Gen. Custer's command or any part of it, in as much as I did not know what companies he had with him. But I saw, about the time Major Reno's command dismounted in the bottom, just as I joined it from the left and front, looking on the bluffs across the river to our right. I saw the gray horse company of the regiment moving down along those bluffs. As I know now the gray horse company was with his command, I know it was Gen. Custer's column.

Q. Did you see anything more than that at that time?

A. No sir.

Q. How long did you look in that direction?

A. I just looked up and saw it. We had plenty to do there and did not look any more.

Q. Did it appear on the crest of the bluff?

A. It was back from the actual edge of the bluffs. The head and the rear of the column were both behind the edge of the bluffs in a sort of hollow, and I just happened to catch sight of about the whole of the gray horse company.

Q. State as near as you can, how far that place was from you; not as you judged it then, but as you became satisfied afterwards.

A. That is difficult to answer. I think they were a little farther down than where we struck the bluffs we came upon them, and not quite so far down as the figure "B" in pencil on the map. They were probably three-fourths of a mile from where we were.

Q. State at what gait that column was moving if you noticed.

A. Gen. Custer generally rode a very fast walking horse that made nearly the whole column trot to keep up with him, and that is my impression of the gait they were moving at.

I, Varnum

Q. State as near as you can how long it was after you saw that gray horse company till Captain Benteen joined Major Reno's command on the top of the hill.

A. About an hour I think.

Q. Bearing in mind the location of the Indian village and the course Gen. Custer's column was taking the last time you saw it, and connecting those facts with the time that had elapsed when Major Reno and Captain Benteen united forces on the hill, state your own belief, or the general belief, as to what point Gen. Custer had reached in reference to the Indian village or the point "B" on the map when Reno's and Benteen's columns united.

A. Gen. Custer must have been in action before that time. I don't know where he would have been but taking into consideration what I learned since, not what I thought at the time, he must have been engaged by that time.

Q. State whether you examined the route or course Gen. Custer took when in the immediate vicinity of the village on the right bank of the river, and how near did his trail come to the point to which Major Reno retreated on the right bank of the stream, describe Gen. Custer's route with reference to that point, with reference to the village, and what developments came under your observation as to the fate of Gen. Custer's command.

A. I can give very little information in answer to that question. We started on the 28th to go down and bury the dead, and in going down I was on a trail which I supposed was Gen. Custer's, and when we got to a high hill that had a pile of stones and Indian medicine bags and other things on it, I went there to see what they were, and rode off the trail and circled around and came back on the trail I suppose near the point "B" in the map. That point was all cut up by pony tracks, and was evidently a watering-place. I went in and watered my horse. Soon after that I had gone out to a ravine and had seen two or three dead bodies when I received orders from Major Reno to go on some bluffs well out from the river with the Indian scouts as a lookout while the men were deployed to bury the dead, and I remained there during the burial.

Q. How far from the place where you watered your horse was it to where you found the dead bodies?

A. I can't give any sort of an opinion. I just remember seeing one body and someone called out "Here are some more," and I was just starting to go there when Major Reno directed me to go on the hills as I have stated. It seems to me it must have been eight hundred or a thousand yards. That is an approximation on my part entirely.

Q. How near to the river was it?

A. I can't locate it any better by that than from the watering-place.

Q. State whether the trail which you supposed to be Gen. Custer's led down to the river.

A. That I don't know. I left the trail some distance back and when I came to that watering-place I did not come on the trail but over a bluff.

Q. Where were the first evidences you found showing that Gen. Custer's command had engaged the Indians and describe those evidences fully.

A. The first evidences were the dead bodies I speak of.

I, Varnum

Q. Were there any evidences showing there had been a struggle there?

A. No sir, only a few dead bodies along in those ravines.

Q. How far was that place where you found the dead bodies from Major Reno's position on the hill, as near as you can tell?

A. I judge about two miles.

Q. Describe the elevation between Major Reno's position on the hill and the point where you found the dead bodies.

A. There were points a little higher than the one where we were, especially pretty well down the river and I think the general lay of the land, the whole surface of the ground was higher than the position where we fought on the hill.

Q. Does it get higher going down the stream?

A. Near where it is the highest it goes right down in a ravine to the river.

Q. State whether you heard the sound of firing in the direction you had seen Gen. Custer's column marching after Major Reno's command took position on the hill; if so describe the firing; its character and duration and to what command it pertained and all you saw or heard with reference to it.

A. About the time, or probably a few minutes after Captain Benteen came up I heard firing from away down the stream, and spoke of it to Lieut. Wallace. I don't recollect any except that one time.

Q. Describe your manner of speaking of it.

A. I had borrowed a rifle of Lieut. Wallace and had

fired a couple of shots at long range, and as I handed the rifle back to him I heard the firing and said: "Jesus Christ! Wallace, hear that! and that!" Those were my words.

Q. How long was that after Captain Benteen's column came up?

A. Very soon after.

Q. Describe that firing.

A. It was not like volley firing but a heavy fire – a sort of crash, crash. I heard it only a few minutes.

Q. To what command did that fire pertain?

A. It must have pertained to Gen. Custer's command at the other end of the Indian village. It was from that end of the village where Gen. Custer's body was afterwards found.

Q. State whether that fire impressed you with anything in regard to Gen. Custer.

A. I thought he was having a warm time down there – a very hot fire evidently.

Q. Go back to the time when Gen. Custer's and Major Reno's commands separated preparatory to Major Reno's advance and state from the course the different columns had taken, as known by you then or afterwards, whether or not it was generally expected or believed when Major Reno's command first engaged the Indians, that any troops would join, support or cooperate with him in his attack upon the Indian village? If so, what troops were expected and what grounds existed, if any, for expecting it?

A. I did not know anything about it. I saw a battalion going into the fight and I went in with it. I don't know what was expected by anybody.

I, Varnum

Q. You have testified about Gen. Custer's column going down the right bank of the river about the time the skirmish line was formed. You must have had some impression about it.

A. I don't know what the expectation was on the part of others, but when I saw a command going on the bluffs, of course I saw some battalion was going to attack the lower end of the village, either from the bluffs or into the village, but how large that command was I did not know.

Q. After Captain Benteen's column had united with Major Reno's on top of the hill who was the senior officer then present?

A. Major Reno.

Q. From the time Major Reno's command first got on the hill and took position there describe particularly the character of the engagement, if any, that there ensued, as to the number of Indians engaged, the severity of the fighting, on the 25th of June, 1876.

A. When we first came up there, there were quite a number of men firing, and I knew from the sound of the shots that there were some Indians around, but no large bodies that I know of.

Q. What was the style of the firing?

A. Just scattering shots here and there. If an Indian came within range he would be fired at.

Q. What was the range of your guns?

A. I don't know the range of a Springfield Carbine, but I think they will shoot pretty accurately for fifteen hundred yards.

Q. Follow that matter down and state in regard to any fighting in that position.

A. There was no other firing going on except what I have described.

Q. Was there an attack on Major Reno's position on the hill that afternoon any time?

A. Yes sir, as I described before. I went to the position of Captain Weir's company at the far point of the ridge down-stream. At that time his men were firing at pretty long range – I should say seven or eight hundred yards – at Indians here and there. At that time I could see all over the plain where towards where I afterwards knew the Custer battlefield had been, and it was just covered with Indians in all directions, coming back towards us.

Q. How much time had elapsed from the time Major Reno had got on the hill till that whole body of Indians you speak of were coming back near enough to begin firing?

A. I should think about two hours.

Q. From the time Major Reno first got up there till the Indians got around him and commenced the general engagement on his position how long was it?

A. Before the entire command on the hill was actually engaged, we had to fight our way back. They had dismounted a skirmish line to cover the retreat and the formation of the lines at the position where we made the stand.

Q. From that time up to the time there became a general engagement, how long was it?

A. Captain Godfrey's company and another company were fighting dismounted some time before, the whole command was actually engaged and it is hard to get an estimate of the time. I should think from the time I was with Captain Weir on that point, back to the time the position was taken on the hill and the line formed where we remained that night was an hour and a half. That is taking in the time of the retreat and formation of the line in position at the time of its deployment into line and getting the packs in.

Q. From the time you saw Captain Weir on the far point to the time Major Reno first took position on the hill, was how long?

A. About two hours. I may be away out of the way in these estimates of time.

Q. Where was Major Reno, what was he doing, and what orders did he give if any from the time his command took position on the hill up to the close of the 25th of June, 1876?

A. I was not near enough to Major Reno to hear him give any orders. The only time I was in position to hear him give an order at all was when we were coming back from that far point I speak of, there was a halt and I heard him say he was going to select a position to make his fight a little farther on. We were moving up stream at the time. That is the only thing I can recollect.

Q. Did you see him frequently during that time?

A. I probably saw him, but I don't recollect.

Q. Did he seem to be directing the movements of the men and exercising the functions of a commanding officer in a great danger?

A. He was with the command and was evidently giving orders from his selecting a site for his position. I was not with any organization, but was riding around, and what orders he did give I did not hear, and would not know about.

Q. From the fact of your riding around would you not be more apt to see the commanding officer than if located at any particular point with his company?

A. Yes sir, I suppose so.

Q. State whether, after Major Reno's command had taken position on the hill, that is after Captain Benteen arrived, there was any solicitude or uneasiness on the part of that command or any part of it as to Gen. Custer's column; if so, state what it was.

A. I suppose everybody felt as I did – wondering what had become of him or where he was. I don't know that there was any special worry; he had five companies with him. I don't think there was an idea or thought in the command that he was in the fix he was.

Q. You testified to certain facts about Major Reno and his three companies in the timber, and yet do I understand you there was no feeling of uneasiness in the command as to the movements of Gen. Custer? I want to get just exactly what the feeling was in the command, and how you felt at that time.

A. There certainly was just that feeling with us. I was thinking: "Has he got in the same fix we are in? What has become of him? Has he been thrown off?" But the idea of the command being cut up and wiped out as it was, I didn't think of such a thing. I don't know as there was any such feeling as that. It was: "What in the world had become of him? Has he been corraled as we are? Has he been thrown off toward the mouth of the river where Gen. Terry's command is?" I can't describe exactly what I felt. There was no feeling that he had been completely used up the way he was. I know I had no such feeling, because when Gen. Terry came up I know the first thing that I and some of the others asked what (was): "Where is Custer? Do you know what has become of Custer?" My impression was that he had been thrown off so he would connect with Gen. Terry's command, he being on the side of the village toward that command, I knowing that command was coming up; and when Gen. Terry's command came up I saw cavalry down in the bottom, and I supposed that he had struck them and hurried them up.

Q. You described certain firing that you heard in that direction. How did that impress you?

A. Well, that he had got to the other end of the village, and struck this force of Indians that we had been fighting, and that he was having a siege of it, too.

Q. The absence of Indians in that interval of time after Major Reno left the woods, and the fact you have testified to of seeing on this plain, or the Custer battlefield, or whatever it was, these vast numbers of Indians coming up, did you reflect and put one thing with another, and see what inference you might draw from that?

A. As we were forming in that position on which we retreated, there was such heavy firing there – that is, we had to catch it so hot immediately afterward – that I don't believe until after the formation of our lines, anybody gave much thought to it.

Q. Did the fact of your seeing Indians leaving you

and going in that direction before the command
took that position impress you in any way?

A. Why, the idea of Custer being killed never struck
me – it never entered my mind.

Q. What do you mean by "Custer?" Do you mean
his command?

A. Yes sir. I mean his command. Anything of that
sort didn't seem to enter my mind at all; and, as
much as I thought of it, I thought they had got
rid of him now, and they were coming back for
us. They first caught us and then him. They had
thrown us back and now they had struck him and
driven him off and were coming back to give us
another dose. That was the idea that struck me.

Q. State, if you know, what was the object of that
movement down the river after Col. Reno and
Captain Benteen had united their forces.

A. I suppose the object of it was to move in the direction of Gen. Custer; that is, knowing that his
command had gone that way, that we were to go
and unite with him.

Q. Do you know whether that was the object?

A. I don't know.

Q. Did you hear any orders given by Major Reno or
any one in regard to it, or did Major Reno say
anything about it?

A. I didn't hear any orders from any person whatever.

Q. You simply supposed the command had gone down
there to see what had become of Gen. Custer?

A. Yes sir. I don't know of anything else that the
movement could have taken that direction for.

Q. You went to Captain Weir's command and started
back from there with it?

A. I didn't start back with him. There was some other

company moving near them. It seemed to me that it was Captain French's company that was there at the time Captain Weir was there. I may be completely wrong about it, but it seems to me there was some company there. I rode along on the flank of that company and then stopped with Captain Moylan when I got back to his company.

Q. State how far the column came with reference to this position of Captain Weir's on that point.

A. The entire command did not come up to where Captain Weir was. There must have been another company there. I know there was another company there with Captain Weir, and the others I don't think were dismounted at all. These two were dismounted and the others came up to very near there, and then the orders to go back or the movement started. Captain Weir started to withdraw his company, I know, and then the remaining portion of the command turned their horses' heads around and went back as he withdrew his line. There was no deployment of the remainder of the line at that position that I know of now at all. They moved up, not in a solid column; each company was a little separate. Some of them might have been along side of each other, and when they came up to near that place – all the companies did not come to the point where Captain Weir was. They may have gone up after I turned back, but I think not; and then they turned and went back.

Q. State what you saw at the time, or which subsequently came to your knowledge, whether the same Indians that engaged Major Reno in the bottom on that day also engaged Gen. Custer's command or vice versa, and what were the evidences that such was the case.

A. They turned from us and went somewhere else. They went back to the other end of the village, and, as Gen. Custer was at the other end of the village and had the fight there, the probability is they were in that fight. I have no doubt of it myself, but that is only my supposition.

Q. From the time Major Reno took his position on the hill until dark on the 25th of June, state whether it was clear or cloudy or calm or windy; if windy, state in what degree and in what direction the wind was blowing with reference to the Custer battlefield, and position of Major Reno on the hill.

A. There was certainly no heavy wind blowing. I don't recollect any. If there had been a heavy wind I would have remembered it; but I think it was a little bit cloudy. It was a little cloudy and I think it sprinkled a little that night – just damp.

Q. State as far as you know what orders or instructions were given on the night of the 25th of June, by Major Reno, describing fully the conduct of that officer as commander of the troops, as far as it came under your observation or notice.

A. The line was first formed. I laind right down on the line with the men while the firing was going on and until it ceased, and as soon as it ceased I was asleep or in a very few minutes afterward. I was exhausted and soon fell asleep and I didn't know anything until the bullets commenced to fly around the next morning, and then I got up. I was lying on a little knoll when the morning came and it was rather exposed, and I started over to Captain French's line, and I laid down in the trench with him. The men had been fortifying during the night, and that was the first sight I had of how they had been throwing up their fortifications, or rather digging out the little holes they did, and that was the first time I noticed exactly where Major Reno was. He was down on Captain Weir's line to the right. I think there were one or two companies intervening between where he was and where Captain French's company was. I presume most of that day I laid with Captain French, or for some little time, there in that hole. I think we were there two or three hours any way. In fact the Indians were firing very rapidly at us, and we just laid still and made no reply to them whatever – just let them shoot – until they would stop to make a rush on us, and then we would get up and open on them and they would go back; and that thing alternated for a long time. About nine or ten o'clock I first went to Captain Moylan's line – on that day I did go to Col. Reno. I endeavored to get some scouts to try and get outside of the lines with a dispatch, and I finally got two or three Crows to say they would go if Rees would go; and I went over to see Col. Reno to get a note, and I think he wrote four copies of the note, and I tried to send it out with the scouts. That was probably on the afternoon of the 26th. The note was not taken out. The Indian scouts did not get through the lines at all. I don't think they made any attempt to at all.

Q. Did the Indians charge your position on the hill?

A. I don't know exactly how to describe the move-
    ment. They would lie behind a ridge from two to
    four or five hundred yards off – as the hills lay
    around us. There was one place where I don't
    think they were a hundred yards off – seventy-five
    or a hundred. We had to charge on them ourselves,
    and drive them out of there, and clear around the
    line it varied to five hundred yards. They would
    lie just behind the ridge and it would be just one
    line of smoke around the whole line. We would
    just lie still and let them go on and when they
    would suppose they had hurt us they would get
    ready and try it on again. They would come up
    and charge us. They would sit back on their horses
    and ride up and we would pour it into them, and
    they would fire back. That was kept up all day
    long.

Q. By whose orders did you charge to get the Indians
    out of their positions?

A. I don't know anything about that. Captain Ben-
    teen had come over and was speaking about his
    line; about having extended his line over further,
    and he said he had to charge to drive them from
    the other end of his knoll, or something like that,
    and he says: "That cuss up there," or something
    like that, "is shooting right into you. We want to
    skip them out." And everybody says: "Is it a go?"
    It's a go," and everybody got up and made a rush.

Q. Who led the charge? Who said is was a go?

A. Almost everybody, we were lying on the line, and
    he said that about this particular Indian on the
    point of this knob – some such remark. I don't
    know that there was any special remark, but it

was, "Is it a go," or some such remark, and then everybody got up and it was a rush; it was not a charge. We ran to this point. We probably went up fifteen or twenty yards, and everybody scattered out of there. We could see the whole outfit skipping out to the hills beyond.

Q. Describe the condition of Major Reno's command on the night of the 25th, and state the causes, if any, you can give for the condition of the command in regard to the number of wounded and other matters, showing in what shape and condition the troops were.

A. I don't know how many wounded we had that night. I didn't go down to where Dr. Porter was with the hospital until some time on the 26th. There may have been twenty, but I don't know how many exactly. The horses and the pack animals were all corraled in a circle, all in together, by tying the reins of about a dozen horses together, and tying them to the legs of the dead horses. They were put in a corral. The corral was covered by Captain Moylan's company behind the pack saddles; and on his left was Col. Weir's company and I think Captain Godfrey's company, and Captain French's company and Lieut. Wallace's company and Captain McDougall's; that is, commencing about the centre of the line, and that took it around to the left, until Captain McDougall's left rested on the river. On the upstream side is a little knoll that is higher than the ground where most of us lay, and on that ground Captain Benteen got his company in line. I don't think the command was in a condition to do any very hard work, more

than they were forced to do under the circumstances, and probably the majority of them slept
that night.

Q. Now in regard to the courage of the command?

A. I think there was plenty of that with the officers
and the troops and everybody. There didn't seem
to be any signs of fear or anything of that sort.

Q. State whether or not Captain Benteen's column
could have united with Major Reno's command
in that timbered place you spoke of.

A. It depends on one thing: From where I saw Captain Benteen's command, if he had crossed the
ford to come up, I don't know how to locate the
time he had to come up if he come up. At the
time we left the timber the Indians turned from
us. Now, if we had remained there and Col. Benteen had started to come in there, what force they
would have put against him is a problem, and
the Indians are the only ones that know anything
about that. When Captain Benteen came up, he
came to us coming down the stream on the right
hand side (bank). From what I understand of the
direction in which he came, he would not have
come in that direction; he would have joined us
probably by the trail on which Col. Reno went
into the woods. I suppose, of course, that not only
the firing, but when he was coming up there
with the Indians, would have attracted him and
he would come in there, unless he had different
orders. Whether the Indians would have force
enough to have attacked him as soon as they saw
him coming, and attacked him on the bottom, and
prevented him from uniting with us, is a question

I cannot answer. If they had sent enough down there, they might have sent him in the timber and prevented him from uniting with us. As the facts were, he certainly could have crossed the river and joined Major Reno, because the Indians turned and went the other way.

Q. Now, in the event that Major Reno had been thus strengthened and re-inforced and in that timber, state whether his position would have been more advantageous and threatening to the Indians, than the position he did take on the hill, and whether or not such position in the timber would have contributed in any way to a junction of his command with that of Gen. Custer, or contributed in any way to the safety of the command?

A. If Col. Benteen had joined Col. Reno in the bottom I suppose you would have taken any troops behind, those of Captain McDougall, – they, of course, would have united in the bottom, – they, of course, could have held the woods for some little time. By putting their forces into the bottom they would certainly have held the bottom for some time, especially as they had the pack train with the ammunition. I mean the position we went out of in the timber. Of course, the presence of our troops as near as we were to the village, would necessarily have kept the force of Indians in our front to fight us; whilst we were there they could not leave their village. That is almost within range of it, and it would have kept a force of Indians there; and as far as forming a junction with Gen. Custer in that direction is concerned, why, we would have had to have formed it by going through the village; either he coming to us or we going to him through the village. I don't believe either party could have gone through the village.

Q. State about the timber down along that left bank below Col. Reno's position.

A. I don't know much about the timber below where we were, because after we buried the dead I came back along this same bank through the timber and went right through the bluffs on the other side of the river. I just rode straight across the village, and I don't know the lay of the land there.

Q. State whether you saw any evidence of any Indian camp being on the right bank of the Little Big Horn river, and if so, where?

A. There had evidently been a village upon the tributary of the Little Big Horn, that we came down in going to the fight. There was an old tepee there and a piece of another tepee, and from the signs around there I should judge there had been a village there, but I don't know how old. I didn't stop to look at it. I should judge that tepee was about a mile from where Col. Reno crossed the river in his advance.

Q. You saw Col. Reno coming back from the river after he had taken that position on the hill?

A. Yes sir.

Q. Was there any special danger in that trip to the river?

A. Well, there was some scattering Indians on the bottom, but no large force there.

Q. When Major Reno's command halted and deployed as skirmishers, state whether the Indians were halted or advancing, or running away from the command at that time?

A. They were evidently attempting to create the impression that they were running away at any rate, and we could see them in among the dust. We could see them not only riding away, but riding back and forth across the valley and mixing up among themselves, and kicking up a dust. I could see the dust receding from in front of us.

Q. Could you tell whether those were mounted Indians or whether they were ponies being driven?

A. I could not tell.

Q. State whether the Indians drove their ponies in any direction, when you got sight of the Indians on the morning of the 25th?

A. When I first saw the Indian ponies I was away back from the river five or six miles or more than that from Major Reno's crossing. I saw them from the high bluffs over there; at that time they were driving the ponies into the village evidently getting the horses to saddle up. The next time I saw the pony-herd was on the 26th. I think I must have seen it on the 25th from the bluffs above, but I don't recollect it. At the time Major Reno's command left the woods, the bulk of the hostile Indians were about five hundred yards from the command. There were several hundred Indians near the village. The largest body of the Indians were nearest the village.

Q. State how many Indians you saw on the bottom, when you left the woods to overtake the troops going out, in the vicinity of the route Major Reno took on his retreat. I mean within range, say one thousand yards.

A. I should think in the timber next to the side I was – that is, next to the river – there were probably twenty-five to thirty Indians; that including those that I saw on the point or the bend there, and from what I could judge there were about a hundred or a hundred and fifty on the other flank at different distances, scattered around riding around there.

Q. State what was the conduct of Major Reno at the Battle of the Little Big Horn in regard to courage and energy and efficiency, whether such as would inspire his men with confidence or the reverse, and state any facts and circumstances in support of your opinion of the conduct of that officer.

A. I can hardly answer that question.

Q. It will have to be answered unless objected to.

A. I certainly have got nothing to say against him and nothing particular for him either one way or the other. That is the whole sum of my answer. What I saw of Col. Reno is what I have described and where I have seen it. I have told where I saw him and what he was doing. In the bottom I saw him with a gun in his hand going with a company of the 7th Cavalry to charge the Indian village. He was deploying the line and forming it; and on top of the hill I just saw exactly what I have said. Certainly there was no sign of cowardice or anything of that sort in his conduct, and nothing specially the other way. I didn't see anything special to say on either side.

Q. That is your answer to the question then is it?

A. Yes, sir, as near as I can answer it.

Q. Were you impressed at the time in the same manner as you speak now?

A. Yes, sir, that was my opinion then.

Q. When was it, if at all, that the mass of the Indians

in the bottom appeared to be moving up the bottom to meet Major Reno's command – before the skirmish line was formed – at the time or before?

A. At the time the skirmish line was formed they kept a certain distance in front of us. When his command was deployed from column of fours into line – the body of Indians seemed to turn back toward us. When we started on again they went on again. They kept a certain distance from us all the time, and we finally halted and dismounted, they turned back again.

Q. State whether you were in a position to see what was going on down the bottom, and describe that position.

A. I was about fifty yards ahead of the column with Lieut. Hare and some of my scouts.

Q. State whether or not the retreat from the timber was hasty, precipitate, disorganized, or the reverse.

A. It was hasty so far as we were concerned, and the rear portion of the column was scattered. Probably the first half of the column was closed up. It was as close as a column of fours moving at a gallop will keep together.

Q. Do you refer to the front or to the whole column?

A. The rear part of the column was strung out to the rear. Take it as a whole, and go away back to the last that came out of the woods, I should think with reference to them they were certainly disorganized – that is the tail end of the column.

Q. State whether or not you really knew at that time from the orders of any officer what was going to be done – I mean at the time you left the skirmish line to catch your horse when you heard those men speak of charging.

A. I didn't know anything about what was going to happen, except that I heard the men hallooing about a charge down in the woods.

Q. What had been the casualties as far as you knew, or as far as you afterward ascertained, at the time that you left the skirmish line to get your horse, and before the men had time to mount?

A. There was some man in "A" company that was left down in the woods that was killed before the command left. I heard people speaking about this man, but I don't remember who he was; I don't know where Sergeant Heyn and this man Strode were shot. One was shot through the knee. He was on his horse when I saw him, but whether he managed to get on the horse with a ball in his knee or not, I don't know. That is all I know about the casualties. I don't know whether Strode and Heyn were shot in the timber or not. The movement from the timber on the retreat I knew was a retreat to get out of there and to get on higher ground somewhere. When I got out on the prairie I was satisfied they were getting away from the Indians as fast as they could.

Q. Was the command driven from the woods by the enemy? Did the enemy enter the woods before the command left it?

A. I don't know whether there were any Indians in the woods or not at the time. I didn't see any in the woods at the time. When we first got a chance to talk about it when we got on the hill, I heard there were Indians behind us in the woods. I heard some of the men say that. They must have meant the timber or bottom that we were in. When I went down to get the horses I had no trouble in getting them. There were no Indians in there where the horses were. Some of the men who had been left as horse-holders were probably firing. They would have been on the skirmish line, too. The line on the left of it was under the same hill that the horses were. All I had to do was to ride down the skirmish line to and beyond the left of the line. Captain Moylan said the Indians were getting in on his left, and the horses were not covered by the skirmish line, and they would probably get in there. I did not see any Indians there when I went to the horses. I didn't see any horses being hit there.

Q. What was your object in trying to overtake the head of the column when it was retreating? Why did you ride so rapidly to overtake the head of the column?

A. I had no special object in mind in going to the head of the column at all. I was foot-loose to go where I liked, and there was the head of the column there, and it was retreating, and I had no more special object than to go where the head of the column was, and if there was anything to be done to help do it; and I had to saw the mouth of my horse to keep him from going ahead of the column. At the head of the column I said something, – "this won't do; this won't do. We have got to get into shape," – or something like that; I don't remember the words. My idea was, thinking that there was no officer there when I got up to the head of the column, to take command of the head of the column myself, and see that it was conducted by somebody. But just as I was saying it I discovered Major Reno there himself, so that my supposition was entirely wrong of thinking there was no one there.

Q. Before the advance had reached the summit of the hill on the retreat, state what efforts you or Major Reno made to check the retreat of the men, and what either of you did for that purpose.

A. I have been told that I said something, but I can't recall it, myself. I don't remember of saying a word. I stopped to get a horse for my orderly and two or three men there helped me to put him on his horse, and I don't remember anything I did or anything anybody else did.

Q. State what were the feelings of the command when it reached the summit of that hill, or in going up there; were the feelings those of triumph and courage and exultation, or those of despondency and demoralization? Was the condition that of a command that had been defeated or that of a command that had made a successful charge?

A. I can't speak for anyone else. I can only speak for myself.

Q. Well, then, speak for yourself.

A. I felt as though I had been pretty badly licked.

The Court then, at 1:30 P.M., adjourned, to meet at 11:00 A.M. tomorrow, Thursday, Jany. 23d, 1879.

[Tenth day.] The examination of Lieut. Varnum by Major Reno was then entered upon as follows:

Q. Please take the map and fix the point where the men were deployed on the skirmish line and its general direction.

A. As this map does not appear to me to be correct, I can't fix it on the map. That square space being the opening in the timber, I should put the skirmish line about the center of that opening as shown on the map. The map may be correct and I may be wrong.

Q. Does the line you have drawn with your pencil represent according to your judgment, the angle of the line?

A. Yes sir; it was about perpendicular to the general direction of the river.

Q. Where were you in reference to the skirmish line at the time it was being deployed?

A. Just as it was being deployed I came right with the men as they were deploying.

Q. Was that the time you saw the Gray Horse Company on the other side of the river?

A. Yes sir.

Q. How long, according to your judgment, did the line remain in the position in which it had been deployed?

A. With reference to that I can only answer that when I came back from the opening in the timber to the skirmish line, the men in the immediate vicinity of where I struck the line were lying in the edge of the timber. I suppose the whole line had dropped back in to the timber, but at what time that happened, I don't know.

Q. What length of time do you compute it to be?

A. I can't tell.

Q. Can you give a judgment of what length of time the men were on the skirmish line before being withdrawn into the timber?

A. I have no idea. I must have been on the skirmish line myself from ten to fifteen minutes.

Q. When you left the skirmish line were the men in the position in which they were deployed?

A. They were.

Q. After they had been withdrawn to the timber how long do you suppose they stayed there?

A. That depends on when they fell back in the timber.

Q. How long were they in the timber altogether? Have you any estimate to give?

A. It could not have been more than ten or fifteen minutes, I think.

Q. How long was it from the time the men were deployed in line till they left the timber on their way back to the river?

A. I estimate that at about half an hour.

Q. Did I understand you to say that a prolongation of the skirmish line across the river would strike the point where you saw the gray horse company?

A. Yes sir I think it was about that point.

Q. Where do you fix that point on the map?

A. I can't fix it on the map. Assuming that the position of Major Reno's command on the hill is correct, it was probably a quarter of a mile below that, or something like that.

Q. Then according to your recollection of the country a prolongation of Major Reno's skirmish line across the river would strike the bluffs about a quarter of a mile below where the stand was made on the night of the 25th?

A. I don't pretend to lay down a rule and say that prolongation of the skirmish line would strike that particular spot where the column was, but I rode in the rear of the skirmish line and looked up there about in front of me was the gray horse company.

Q. Did you not go rather on the right of Major Reno's command than in the rear of the skirmish line?

A. That is what I say: As I came in from the left of the line and rode around in the rear, I looked up there it was in my front which would be about at the right flank of the line as it was deployed.

Q. What was the character of the country on which you saw the gray horse company?

A. It was up on the bluffs we afterwards retreated to and when we had our fight. It was rather rough. That is the top was uneven and rolling. It was a high bluff.

Q. Much higher than the point from which you saw it?

A. Yes sir; I think the bluffs were a hundred feet high.

Q. That was the last view you had of that column or any part of it?

A. That was the last view I ever had of it, and that was just a glance.

Q. Major Reno deployed his skirmish line and they remained ten or fifteen minutes in position?

A. Yes sir.

Q. These men had dismounted at the time?

A. Yes sir. I think they were just coming from their horses at the time I rode up.

Q. Was that point at which the line was deployed visible from the point where the gray horse company was visible to you at the time you saw it?

A. It must have been.

Q. Did you tell Major Reno, while in the timber or

at any time during the general engagement, about seeing the gray horse company?

A. No sir.

Q. Where was Major Reno in reference to yourself at that time?

A. I don't know; he must have been on the line as the men were just deploying.

Q. You spoke of seeing Major Reno with a gun in his hand; did any of the officers enter that fight with sabers or swords?

A. Not that I know of. I almost know there was not a saber in the command.

Q. What was the gait you fixed at which the gray horse company was moving down the river?

A. I think they were moving at a trot. That is an impression only; not a very fast trot.

Q. What was the general appearance of the point "B" in the river, as to its being a ford or not?

A. I should call that place a ford. I did not attempt to cross the river there, but I should call it a ford.

Q. What do you estimate the distance from the point "B" and the place where you saw the gray horse company?

A. I should put it at something less than two miles. All my testimony in relation to time and distance is very uncertain.

Q. How long do you suppose it would take a command going at the rate that appeared to be going to go from the point where you saw it to "B"?

A. Taking into consideration the uneven nature of the ground, it must have taken them twenty-five or thirty minutes, assuming that my distance is about correct.

I, Varnum

Q. Do you know whether the gray horse company was at the head, the middle or the rear of that column?

A. I have no idea.

Q. What was the character of the country between the point where the gray horse company was and the point "B" with reference to access or approach to the river, on the right bank?

A. Some parts it must have been just about impossible to get down with a company of cavalry, and at other points you could go down quite well.

Q. Would it be as easy for a column of mounted men to go down the right bank to the river as for any number of mounted men on the left bank to rise to those heights?

A. Certainly it would be fully as easy to go down as to get up.

Q. How long after you saw the gray horse company as you have stated till Major Reno retreated from the timber?

A. It must have been about half an hour.

Q. Then according to your estimate of time a sufficient period had elapsed between the time you saw the gray horse company and the time Major Reno left the timber for that column to have reached the ford "B".

A. Yes sir, just about.

Q. In what way did the Indians leave Major Reno's command after he made the march across the river on his return; down towards the village or not?

A. Down towards the village.

Q. That was on the left side of the river, down towards "B"?

A. Yes sir.

Q. When did they leave Major Reno's command?

A. I think the main force left about the time we left the woods.

Q. Then according to your judgment at the time Major Reno's command left the timber Gen. Custer's column had about time enough to have reached the ford "B"?

A. I think those would have been the relative positions of the two columns as near as I can judge.

Q. What was the character of the country as to elevation between the point where you saw the gray horse company and the point "B", whether the point where you saw the gray horse company was as high as any point between that and "B"?

A. I hardly think it was. I can't be accurate.

Q. I wish to ask your judgment. You saw the gray horse company at the point you have stated. The men of Major Reno's command were just being deployed or had been dismounted and deployed as a skirmish line. They remained there for ten minutes. Do you suppose the column moving down the right bank of the stream could have seen Major Reno's command in any other position than on the skirmish line with dismounted men?

A. I will answer that in this way. As this column of Gen. Custer's went down the stream, he may have been in a position to see us all the time we were going down the bottom, but at the time he passed the point I have described we were certainly dismounting and he must have known our position if he looked there. That was what we were doing.

Q. Any stretch of country over which he passed for the next ten or fifteen minutes would still have been in view of Major Reno's skirmish line?

I, Varnum

A. The last I saw of the gray horse company Gen. Custer was himself, if he rode at the head of the column as usual, in a position to see what we were doing.

Q. Then, as far as you have any reason to believe, the last view the column on the right bank of the river had of Major Reno's command was doing what?

A. Dismounting to go into the fight.

Q. Was there any communication whatever to your knowledge between Major Reno and Gen. Custer after that time?

A. Not that I know of. I don't believe there was.

Q. Then as far as you know Gen. Custer must have reached the point "B", if he attempted to cross there at all, with the belief that Major Reno wasn't charging, but standing there at bay before the Indians?

A. Of course I can't say positively; it is a mere matter of opinion. The men of the gray horse company were certainly in position to see exactly what we were doing there. What part of the column the gray horse company was in I don't know, or how far ahead of the gray horse company Gen. Custer was, I don't know. But assuming he was right there, he must have seen our position and known exactly what we were doing.

Q. Do you suppose that Gen. Custer as a careful soldier having an opportunity to see that command in the timber below there would advise himself of just what it was doing and the position and the condition it was in?

A. I believe Gen. Custer must have been satisfied to proceed after seeing us there.

Q. Have you any reason to think that Gen. Custer

168

had any other knowledge of Major Reno than that he was standing there on his defense?

A. If he saw us there, and I can't help thinking he did see us, that must have been the last information he had concerning us.

Q. Were there any evidences of a determined effort – to cross to the village at "B"?

A. I don't know anything about that. I did not watch the ground there at all. I came over the bluff at that point, and not on the trail.

Q. As a military man would not your attention have been attracted if there had been any evidences of a struggle on the part of Gen. Custer to cross to the village at the point "B"?

A. Gen. Custer might have attempted to cross at "B" and have been driven back without leaving any particular signs except horse-tracks, unless some one had been killed or wounded there so that he would have dead bodies or dead horses there. I did not see any dead bodies or dead horses to indicate any struggle, though he may have gone in there.

Q. There were men left dead in the timber where Major Reno made his stand?

A. Yes sir.

Q. Would there not have been men and horses left dead at "B" if there had been a desperate effort to cross?

A. Yes sir, I think so.

Q. How far from that ford did you find the first dead body?

A. My opinion of that distance is the poorest opinion I give. I said eight hundred or a thousand yards, but it is a complete guess on my part.

I, Varnum

Q. It was away from the ford was it?

A. Yes sir.

Q. And still farther down the river?

A. Yes sir; it was after I left the ford.

Q. It was not between the position Major Reno took when he came on the hill and the ford "B"?

A. No sir.

Q. Then you say for about thirty minutes Major Reno remained in the timber and created a diversion on the part of the Indians.

A. Yes sir.

Q. According to your estimate of the number of Indians engaged on the 25th and 26th days of June, 1876, were there not enough in your opinion to have overcome both commands even if each had been separately engaged at the same time?

A. I would not like to take half the warriors and take the command we had with us and fight them.

Q. You would not like to take the other half of the of the command and fight the balance of the warriors?

A. No sir. I don't know how to express an opinion on that. From the estimates of other persons and of Indians and all I can pick up, I don't believe there were less than four thousand warriors in that fight.

Q. Were there any evidences of an attempt on the part of the column under Gen. Custer to return from the point "B" back in the direction from which he came?

A. I did not notice any evidences of that sort and if there had been I would not have noticed them as I rode away from the trail.

Q. What was the character of the country from the

point "B" in the direction of "D" and "E" as to
elevation in comparison with the position of Major
Reno's command on the night of the 25th?

A. I have no idea; I never was on either of these
points except to pass by where Gen. Custer's body
was buried when I came in from the bluffs.

Q. Did you see the bodies before they were buried?

A. I saw a great many bodies but not to examine them.

Q. Did the position of the bodies indicate that the
command had been gathered together in a military position at any point for resistance to the
Indians?

A. It is impossible for me to give an opinion on that.
I was not enough over the field to know.

Q. When the column under command of Major Reno
prepared to retire from the bottom were you with
Girard and Reynolds?

A. Yes sir.

Q. They were unattached to any particular part of
the command were they not?

A. Yes sir. The interpreter, as a rule, is supposed to
be with the commanding officer.

Q. Was he with him at that time?

A. No sir. I wish to say that I had no orders to go
with Major Reno's command at all, and I don't
know what instructions Girard had, nor do I know
how he came to be there.

Q. You were with these two men, who were, as far
as you know unattached to any particular part of
the command?

A. Yes sir.

Q. When the men were in the timber were they not
a small number of men to defend a position of
that kind?

I, Varnum

A. I don't believe we had enough men to cover as large a line as it was necessary to cover in order to hold the timber. It does not seem so to me.

Q. You have been asked several questions with reference to the ability of Major Reno's command to hold that timber provided Captain Benteen with his command had joined and provided Captain McDougall had come in with the packtrain. Would not that in your judgment depend on the fact whether there had been any orders or directions to Major Reno and Captain Benteen to unite their commands?

A. It would depend entirely upon the fact whether they did or not; and whether they would or not would depend of course on the orders each one had, more or less. I don't know what orders either one had.

Q. Was it reasonable for Major Reno to expect Captain Benteen's command to unite with his on that side of the river unless he was apprised of the fact that Captain Benteen had been ordered to do so? In other words must he not know what Captain Benteen was ordered to do before he could calculate on what he would do?

A. I do not see how he could depend on Captain Benteen's command or Captain McDougall's. I don't know whether Major Reno knew or could have known what orders the other battalion commanders had. I do not know that he knew what the plan of the fight was; I did not.

Q. If Major Reno was ignorant of the orders given to Captain Benteen with his battalion, and to Captain McDougall with the packtrain, would he have been justified in holding that timber in the belief that they would come up and unite with him, provided he found or believed his own command was not sufficient to hold it?

A. If he believed he was unable to hold that timber and saw no troops coming in, I suppose he would use his own judgment about leaving there and going to some place he could hold better.

Q. How long after retiring from the timber did Captain Benteen unite with him?

A. I would say twenty or twenty-five minutes.

Q. How long after Captain Benteen came up did the packtrain come up, and did it come from the same direction that Captain Benteen did or a different one?

A. It came from a different direction and I estimate it three-quarters of an hour, possible more or less.

Q. After the packtrain joined the command, how long till the entire command moved down the river?

A. After the packtrain joined the command, I took the spades and started down the hill, and was gone possibly twenty or twenty-five minutes, and when I got back the command was all moving except perhaps Captain Moylan's company, which I am not certain about, as he was encumbered with wounded.

Q. Where was Company "D", under Captain Weir at that time?

A. I can't locate his company at that time. I know some company started forward about the time I went down the hill, but whether it was his or not I don't know.

Q. What time do you fix it with reference to the time the packtrain came up?

I, Varnum

A. It was just about the time the packtrain came up.

Q. How long did Major Reno remain on the hill before the column moved down the river?

A. I guess it was about on hour and a half before the whole thing started.

Q. Did you see the point at which Captain Weir halted after he moved down the river?

A. Yes sir, I was on that point.

Q. Was it possible for the column to have got any farther in that direction, having reference to the number of Indians and their position?

A. I can only speak in reference to the time I got there. Then the whole force of Indians seemed to be turning back against us. It is possible that we could have gone farther, but I doubt whether anyone would have moved any farther at that time, because the Indians were all coming as fast as they could in our direction.

Q. Was not the engagement a general one after the time Captain Weir commenced to return with his company until dark that evening?

A. No, not from the time he commenced to return. But he had to keep firing to keep the Indians at a distance and it got warmer and warmer till we got back and from that time on it was a very heavy fire as long as we could see to shoot.

Q. What do you fix as the time you reached the point where you made the stand that night?

A. About half past five o'clock is as near as I can fix it.

Q. When you heard the firing in the direction in which you afterwards found Gen. Custer did you communicate that fact to Major Reno?

A. No sir.

Q. Was not General Terry known to be advancing up the river with a considerable body of soldiers?

A. I don't know whether it was generally known or not. I partly knew what General Terry's intentions were, as I had heard him and Gen. Custer talking, and I had an idea Gen. Terry was on the Big Horn somewhere, but I don't know exactly how I knew it either.

Q. Was it not a matter of belief throughout the command, as far as the officers were concerned, that Gen. Terry was coming up the river with a column of men?

A. I don't know how much information there was among the officers.

Q. Was there anything in the amount of firing you heard in the direction in which Gen. Custer's command was afterwards found, to indicate their destruction at that time?

A. No sir, I had no idea the command had been destroyed.

Q. Was it not the general belief that the command of Gen. Custer was as well able to take care of itself as that of Major Reno as far as you knew the feeling?

A. I can't recall anyone speaking about it till the afternoon of the 26th.

Q. Was it not a belief among the officers that he was as well able to take care of his command as the command of Major Reno to take care of itself?

A. I have no idea what the officers thought about that.

Q. Was it not the belief or opinion that he might have gone farther down the river in the direction in which Gen. Terry was expected to advance and so unite with him?

A. I certainly had an idea myself that he had been driven off in his attack on the other end of the village, and that he was either corraled, as we were, in the hills, or had got away towards Gen. Terry's command. The idea of their being all killed never struck me at all.

Q. You spoke of an attempt on the part of Major Reno to send a letter to Gen. Terry?

A. Yes sir; on the 26th.

Q. Was that letter returned to him by the Indian scouts?

A. Yes sir.

Q. Do you remember the substance of that letter? Major Reno stating to the Court that the letter has been destroyed and he is unable now to produce it.

A. It stated in effect that he had arrived at that point at such a time, describe the location on the hill, that we had attacked the Indians; that he did not know the whereabouts of General Custer; that he was holding the Indians in check, and asked for medical aid and assistance. That is about all I remember of the letter.

Q. Did he speak of his ability to hold the position?

A. My impression is it did say something to that effect. Yet, I don't feel certain of it.

Q. Do you or not recollect he said something like this: — we are able to hold the position but we have a number of wounded and I would like you to send me some medical stores and supplies?

A. I don't think it was exactly like that. I think it was: "we require medical aid and assistance," or something like that. There was something about holding the position but I don't recollect how it was worded; it was to the effect that he was able to hold it.

Q. Was it not, as far as you recollect, very much in substance like a letter he wrote on the 27th?

A. I don't know anything about the letter he wrote on the 27th. I have been shown a letter that seems to have been written on the 27th. That one is in substance about the same as the one I saw, with the addition of occurrences which had happened after he wrote the first one.

Q. There was no substantial difference as to his ability to remain where he was and his ignorance of the whereabouts of Gen. Custer?

A. No sir. Those things were about the same in both letters.

Q. That firing you heard was after Captain Benteen came up?

A. I think it was very soon after he came up.

Q. Was the range of the Indians' rifles greater or less than that of the soldiers' carbines?

A. I believe the longest range guns the Indians had were those they took from Gen. Custer's command, with one or two exceptions. There were one or two parties in particular (that) had very long range guns.

Q. Is the range of the Winchester rifle the same as the army carbine?

A. No sir, I think it is much less.

Q. What is the range of the Winchester rifle?

A. I don't know exactly. I think the charge of powder is considerably less than that of the Springfield carbine.

Q. The Indians in going to the river and across it to

the right bank, would in all probability cross at "B"?

A. I don't know; there were other fords close there.

Q. Was not "B" the first ford they could cross?

A. It is the lowest ford in the vicinity of the village.

Q. Is there any ford between that and the point you crossed in the retreat from the bottom?

A. I don't know. I don't believe there is because it is high bluffs, but I was never through there.

Questions by the Recorder

Q. Refresh your memory, in hunting on the plains, and see if you can't get at the range of a Winchester rifle?

A. The Winchester Arms Company has an arm very different from the old Winchester rifle. I don't think the Winchester will shoot accurately over six hundred yards. With regard to the fifteen hundred yards range of the carbine, I did not mean that it would shoot accurately that distance, but that it would throw a ball that far.

Q. How far will a Springfield carbine shoot with reasonable accuracy?

A. About a thousand yards.

Q. State if you had been in Indian engagements before that.

A. Yes sir.

Q. Is it the habit of the plains Indians to charge an enemy posted in the timber? Would they be likely to do it?

A. I don't believe they would be likely to come there mounted, but any place an Indian can cover himself he will take advantage of and crawl up on the line.

Q. The troops were in the timber and had the cover as you have testified?

A. Yes sir.

Q. Did the Indians on the plain have cover?

A. Not on the plain but they had the advantage of timber above and below us on the stream.

Q. In that particular timber they did not come that you saw?

A. I saw no Indians in that particular timber I was in.

Q. State whether the plains Indians are more likely to charge a retreating foe than one ready for the attack. What is the rule in regard to that in that country?

A. I think that applies to the Indian and to the cavalry too – they would rather strike a man when he is retreating than when he is facing you. I had.

Q. Did not the Indians strike Major Reno's column when it left the timber, and were not the greatest number of casualties occasioned in that way?

A. I think a great number of casualties must have occurred in the timber, just as we left in the rear of the column. Certainly the greater number were killed and wounded in the retreat from the woods to the bluff and about the ford. I don't know exactly where they were killed or how. Some must have been killed near the timber as we left, and some must have been left there, I am not certain.

Q. State whether or not the Indians made a charge into Major Reno's column; into the rear or tail end of it as it left the woods on the retreat?

I, Varnum

A. They did not charge into it. They would ride some distance off on the flank – some fifty to a hundred yards, with their rifles across the pommels of their saddles, and would sit there and work their rifles.

Q. Not bringing them to the shoulder?

A. No sir; let them lay across their saddles.

Q. Did they follow the command in that way as it went down the bottom?

A. A great many followed down, but as we neared the river they commenced to draw off the other way.

Q. State whether or not the movement of Major Reno's battalion from the woods to the hill was a demoralized rout.

A. I do not consider the head of the column was in that condition. The rear I think was.

Q. Do you still hold to the opinion that in column of fours is a good formation in which to charge an enemy in front? Would that have been a good formation there at that time?

A. In column of fours is a good formation in an attempt to pass through a column of Indians. The object of that movement was to take us outside of a body of Indians, and that was as good a formation as any. If it had been made in platoon it would have caused delay.

Q. The formation depends on the rapidity with which you wished to move?

A. Yes sir, and what the effect of the movement was to be.

Q. Take those Indians between the command and the ford, and the command starting out in a column of fours, would it or not be likely to receive an enfilading fire, or a fire from the head of the column down?

A. In fighting Indians I don't think it would. They would try to get on the flanks where they could use their guns as I have described. That is their style of fighting. I would make the formation close and if the object was to break through a lot of Indians I don't know but it would be a good way to go.

Q. Was that done?

A. The rear of the column was certainly not closed up.

Q. Where did you expect to find the commanding officer on the retreat?

A. At the head of the column.

Q. Was there any officer at the rear of the column, as it came out of the woods seeing that the men all got out?

A. There were officers back there: I don't know what they were doing. I think Lieut. Hodgson, Lieut. Wallace, Captain French and Lieut. McIntosh were all behind me.

Q. Was the column in front going?

A. Yes sir.

Q. At the point where you came out of the woods how was the column scattered or formed?

A. I could not get out as long as it was closed up solid because that forced me into the woods, but as soon as there was a break in the column I got out.

Q. When you got out there were still men behind you?

A. Yes sir.

Q. Were there any wounded men left in the woods?

I, Varnum

A. I don't know whether there were or not. There were men left there, and when we saw them they were dead.

Q. Is it reasonable to suppose that every man you saw was shot dead in the first instance or wounded?

A. I don't know about that. I think if a man was disabled so he could not get on his horse (he) was left where he was.

Q. Then what would be liable to become of him?

A. He would be liable to be killed at once.

Q. How many were killed or left in the woods?

A. I don't know. Some were on the plain and some in the woods.

Q. From the place where the skirmish line was formed, was any charge made towards the Indian village by Major Reno's command or was any such order given by him?

A. No sir, no charge out on the plain. The only charge I know anything about was the movement Major Reno started to make with Company "G" through the woods which I understood was towards a part of the Indian village.

Q. Within what limits have you heard the force of Indians there placed?

A. I don't think I have heard it placed at less than twenty-five hundred, and as high as twelve thousand warriors.

Q. From your knowledge of Indians, state what would be the population of a village containing four thousand warriors?

A. About fifteen thousand if they all had their families with them. I don't believe they all had their families. I saw a great many wickyups, which probably contained bucks only.

Q. Were any of those wickyups alongside of the lodges?

A. I did not go over the ground enough to see how they were. At the lower end of the village a great many were left standing.

Q. Have you ever seen wickyups alongside of lodges, put there for a special purpose?

A. Yes sir, for bath houses, I suppose you refer to.

Q. Are they not there for other purposes – for the women to occupy occasionally?

A. I don't know. The only use I know of their making of them is for their sweat baths.

Q. About how many ponies would it take to move a village of fifteen thousand Indians with all the plunder the Indians have?

A. I don't know how to estimate that. It would take a great many, and there was an immense herd of ponies there. If there were that number of Indians it would require about twenty thousand ponies.

Q. What was the size of the moving village if you saw it?

A. I did not see it. I wish to say in regard to the number of ponies that, when I was on the bluffs the night before my Indian scouts said there were more ponies than they ever saw together before – that they looked like an immense buffalo herd. I could not see them at all. They told me to look for worms on the ground, but still I could not see the ponies, but they described them as the largest pony herd they had ever seen.

Q. What became of your Indian scouts?

A. I think they started for Powder River. I found them there afterwards.

Q. When a fight is going on, and an officer in charge

of a column has no orders to remain away or at a certain position, and he hears the sound of firing what is it his duty to do always?

A. I suppose he would take his command and go there to find out what was going on and help or send and find out what the matter was.

Q. Was not Captain Benteen's column doing that, if you know, when Major Reno's column got up on the hill?

A. A few minutes after we got on the hill I saw a column of cavalry coming down stream towards us. I don't know where it had been before, or what it had been doing.

Q. In the event that one thousand Indians had followed Major Reno's column, and had closed up on it at the river when the men were going across and trying to get on the hill, what would have been the result as far as that command was concerned?

A. I don't think it could ever have got on the hill. I think it would have stopped at the creek.

Questions by Major Reno

Q. You are a soldier and I presume you remember the soldierly performance of Gen. Forsyth on the Republican river in 1869?

A. Yes sir.

Q. Were the Indians charging upon the troops at that time, and after Gen. Forsyth had been in the timber one day?

A. I was not there, but that is what I understand was the nature of the fight there. I don't know the nature of their charge on the troops. I imagine the charge of the Indians is not the same as of the cavalry. I think I understand what is meant by a charge there.

Q. Does not the method of Indian warfare depend on the number of Indians and the number of troops against whom they are engaged?

A. Yes sir.

Q. Are not their tactics modified by circumstances?

A. Yes sir, every Indian fights for himself and each one has his own way of doing it.

Q. And that way depends on their numbers and the number of their enemy?

A. Yes sir.

Q. Was that or not a proper formation for Major Reno's column in going to a narrow ford in retreating from the timber to the top of the hill beyond having in view the distance?

A. I don't know that it would make any difference whether the ford was narrow or wide as far as the formation was concerned. In a movement of that sort, the line has to be kept well closed up all the time, and if there is any delay in crossing the ford, some disposition would have to be made to cover the delay.

Q. Was not that a proper formation of the command, to go to the point to which it was directed?

A. I think it was.

Q. Major Reno was at the head of the command?

A. Yes sir.

Q. (By the Recorder). Do you know whether the Indians got away with General Forsyth there?

A. No, they did not.

Q. (By Major Reno). Nor with Major Reno?

A. No sir.

End of Varnum Testimony

Index

The Chronological Biographical Listing of Varnum's life has not been indexed. Footnotes are indicated by an "n" following the page number.

I, Varnum